William Shakespeare

THE
TWO GENTLEMEN
OF VERONA

Edited by Bertrand Evans

The Signet Classic Shakespeare
GENERAL EDITOR: SYLVAN BARNET

PUBLISHED BY THE NEW AMERICAN LIBRARY, NEW YORK
AND
THE NEW ENGLISH LIBRARY LIMITED, LONDON

822·3

**This book is to be returned on or before
the last date stamped below.**

Contents

Shakespeare: Prefatory Remarks

Between the record of his baptism in Stratford on 26 April 1564 and the record of his burial in Stratford on 25 April 1616, some forty documents name Shakespeare, and many others name his parents, his children, and his grandchildren. More facts are known about William Shakespeare than about any other playwright of the period except Ben Jonson. The facts should, however, be distinguished from the legends. The latter, inevitably more engaging and better known, tell us that the Stratford boy killed a calf in high style, poached deer and rabbits, and was forced to flee to London, where he held horses outside a playhouse. These traditions are only traditions; they may be true, but no evidence supports them, and it is well to stick to the facts.

Mary Arden, the dramatist's mother, was the daughter of a substantial landowner; about 1557 she married John Shakespeare, who was a glove-maker and trader in various farm commodities. In 1557 John Shakespeare was a member of the Council (the governing body of Stratford), in 1558 a constable of the borough, in 1561 one of the two town chamberlains, in 1565 an alderman (entitling him to the appellation "Mr."), in 1568 high bailiff—the town's highest political office, equivalent to mayor. After 1577, for an unknown reason he drops out of local politics. The birthday of William Shakespeare, the eldest son of this locally prominent man, is unrecorded; but the Stratford parish register records that the infant was baptized on 26 April 1564. (It is quite possible that he was born on 23

April, but this date has probably been assigned by tradition because it is the date on which, fifty-two years later, he died.) The attendance records of the Stratford grammar school of the period are not extant, but it is reasonable to assume that the son of a local official attended the school and received substantial training in Latin. The masters of the school from Shakespeare's seventh to fifteenth years held Oxford degrees; the Elizabethan curriculum excluded mathematics and the natural sciences but taught a good deal of Latin rhetoric, logic, and literature. On 27 November 1582 a marriage license was issued to Shakespeare and Anne Hathaway, eight years his senior. The couple had a child in May, 1583. Perhaps the marriage was necessary, but perhaps the couple had earlier engaged in a formal "troth plight" which would render their children legitimate even if no further ceremony were performed. In 1585 Anne Hathaway bore Shakespeare twins.

That Shakespeare was born is excellent; that he married and had children is pleasant; but that we know nothing about his departure from Stratford to London, or about the beginning of his theatrical career, is lamentable and must be admitted. We would gladly sacrifice details about his children's baptism for details about his earliest days on the stage. Perhaps the poaching episode is true (but it is first reported almost a century after Shakespeare's death), or perhaps he first left Stratford to be a schoolteacher, as another tradition holds; perhaps he was moved by

> Such wind as scatters young men through the world,
> To seek their fortunes further than at home
> Where small experience grows.

In 1592, thanks to the cantankerousness of Robert Greene, a rival playwright and a pamphleteer, we have our first reference, a snarling one, to Shakespeare as an actor and playwright. Greene warms those of his own educated friends who wrote for the theater against an actor who has presumed to turn playwright:

There is an upstart crow, beautified with our feathers, that with his *tiger's heart wrapped in a player's hide* supposes he is as well able to bombast out a blank verse as the best of you, and being an absolute Johannes-factotum is in his own conceit the only Shake-scene in a country.

The reference to the player, as well as the allusion to Aesop's crow (who strutted in borrowed plumage, as an actor struts in fine words not his own), makes it clear that by this date Shakespeare had both acted and written. That Shakespeare is meant is indicated not only by "Shake-scene" but by the parody of a line from one of Shakespeare's plays, *3 Henry VI:* "O, tiger's heart wrapped in a woman's hide." If Shakespeare in 1592 was prominent enough to be attacked by an envious dramatist, he probably had served an apprenticeship in the theater for at least a few years.

In any case, by 1592 Shakespeare had acted and written, and there are a number of subsequent references to him as an actor: documents indicate that in 1598 he is a "principal comedian," in 1603 a "principal tragedian," in 1608 he is one of the "men players." The profession of actor was not for a gentleman, and it occasionally drew the scorn of university men who resented writing speeches for persons less educated than themselves, but it was respectable enough: players, if prosperous, were in effect members of the bourgeoisie, and there is nothing to suggest that Stratford considered William Shakespeare less than a solid citizen. When, in 1596, the Shakespeares were granted a coat of arms, the grant was made to Shakespeare's father, but probably William Shakespeare (who the next year bought the second-largest house in town) had arranged the matter on his own behalf. In subsequent transactions he is occasionally styled a gentleman.

Although in 1593 and 1594 Shakespeare published two narrative poems dedicated to the Earl of Southampton, *Venus and Adonis* and *The Rape of Lucrece,* and may well have written most or all of his sonnets in the middle nineties, Shakespeare's literary activity seems to have been almost entirely devoted to the theater. (It may be significant that the two narrative poems were written in years when the plague closed the theaters for several months.) In 1594 he was a charter member of a theatrical company called the Chamberlain's Men (which in 1603 changed its name to the King's Men); until he retired to Stratford (about 1611, apparently), he was with this remarkably stable company. From 1599 the company acted primarily at the Globe Theatre, in which Shakespeare held a one-tenth interest. Other Elizabethan dramatists are known to have acted, but no other is known also to have been entitled to a share in the profits of the playhouse.

Shakespeare's first eight published plays did not have his name on them, but this is not remarkable; the most popular play of the sixteenth century, Thomas Kyd's *The Spanish Tragedy,* went through many editions without naming Kyd, and Kyd's authorship is known only because a book on the profession of acting happens to quote (and attribute to Kyd) some lines on the interest of Roman emperors in the drama. What is remarkable is that after 1598 Shakespeare's name commonly appears on printed plays—some of which are not his. Another indication of his popularity comes from Francis Meres, author of *Palladis Tamia: Wit's Treasury* (1598): in this anthology of snippets accompanied by an essay on literature, many playwrights are mentioned, but Shakespeare's name occurs more often than any other, and Shakespeare is the only playwright whose plays are listed.

From his acting, playwriting, and share in a theater, Shakespeare seems to have made considerable money. He put it to work, making substantial investments in Stratford real estate. When he made his will (less than a month before he died), he sought to leave his property intact to his descendants. Of small bequests to relatives and to friends (including three actors, Richard Burbage, John Heminges, and Henry Condell), that to his wife of the second-best bed has provoked the most comment; perhaps it was the bed the couple had slept in, the best being reserved for visitors. In any case, had Shakespeare not excepted it, the bed would have gone (with the rest of his household possessions) to his daughter and her husband. On 25 April 1616 he was buried within the chancel of the church at Stratford. An unattractive monument to his memory, placed on a wall near the grave, says he died on 23 April. Over the grave itself are the lines, perhaps by Shakespeare, that (more than his literary fame) have kept his bones undisturbed in the crowded burial ground where old bones were often dislodged to make way for new:

> Good friend, for Jesus' sake forbear
> To dig the dust enclosèd here.
> Blessed be the man that spares these stones
> And cursed be he that moves my bones.

Thirty-seven plays, as well as some nondramatic poems, are held to constitute the Shakespeare canon. The dates of composition of most of the works are highly uncertain, but there is often evidence of a *terminus a quo* (starting point) and/or a *terminus ad quem* (terminal point) that provides a framework for intelligent guessing. For example, *Richard II* cannot be earlier than 1595, the publication date of some material to which it is indebted; *The Merchant of Venice* cannot be later than 1598, the year Francis Meres mentioned it. Sometimes arguments for a date hang on an alleged topical allusion, such as the lines about the unseasonable weather in *A Midsummer Night's Dream,* II.i.81–87, but such an allusion (if indeed it is an allusion) can be variously interpreted, and in any case there is always the possibility that a topical allusion was inserted during a revision, years after the composition of a play. Dates are often attributed on the basis of style, and although conjectures about style usually rest on other conjectures, sooner or later one must rely on one's literary sense. There is no real proof, for example, that *Othello* is not as early as *Romeo and Juliet,* but one feels *Othello* is later, and because the first record of its performance is 1604, one is glad enough to set its composition at that date and not push it back into Shakespeare's early years.

The following chronology, then, is as much indebted to informed guesswork and sensitivity as it is to fact. The dates, necessarily imprecise, indicate something like a scholarly consensus.

PLAYS

1609–10	*Cymbeline*
1610–11	*The Winter's Tale*
1611	*The Tempest*
1612–13	*Henry VIII*

POEMS

1592	*Venus and Adonis*
1593–94	*The Rape of Lucrece*
1593–1600	*Sonnets*
1600–01	*The Phoenix and Turtle*

Shakespeare's Theater

In Shakespeare's infancy, Elizabethan actors performed wherever they could—in great halls, at court, in the courtyards of inns. The innyards must have made rather unsatisfactory theaters: on some days they were unavailable because carters bringing goods to London used them as depots; when available, they had to be rented from the innkeeper; perhaps most important, London inns were subject to the Common Council of London, which was not well disposed toward theatricals. In 1574 the Common Council required that plays and playing places in London be licensed. It asserted that

> sundry great disorders and inconveniences have been found to ensue to this city by the inordinate haunting of great multitudes of people, specially youth, to plays, interludes, and shows, namely occasion of frays and quarrels, evil practices of incontinency in great inns having chambers and secret places adjoining to their open stages and galleries,

and ordered that innkeepers who wished licenses to hold performances put up a bond and make contributions to the poor.

The requirement that plays and innyard theaters be licensed, along with the other drawbacks of playing at inns, probably drove James Burbage (a carpenter-turned-actor) to rent in 1576 a plot of land northeast of the city walls and to build here—on property outside the jurisdiction of the city—England's first permanent construction designed for plays. He called it simply the Theatre. About all that is known of its construction is that it was wood. It soon had imitators, the most famous being the Globe (1599), built across the Thames (again outside the city's jurisdiction), out of timbers of the Theatre, which had been dismantled when Burbage's lease ran out.

There are three important sources of information about the structure of Elizabethan playhouses — drawings, a contract, and stage directions in plays. Of drawings, only the so-called De Witt drawing (c. 1596) of the Swan—really a friend's copy of De Witt's drawing—is of much significance. It shows a building of three tiers, with a stage jutting from a wall into the yard or center of the building. The tiers are roofed, and part of the stage is covered by a roof that projects from the rear and is supported at its front on two posts, but the groundlings, who paid a penny to stand in front of the stage, were exposed to the sky. (Performances in such a playhouse were held only in the daytime; artificial illumination was not used.) At the rear of the stage are two doors; above the stage is a gallery. The second major source of information, the contract for the Fortune, specifies that although the Globe is to be the model, the Fortune is to be square, eighty feet outside and fifty-five inside. The stage is to be forty-three feet broad, and is to extend into the middle of the yard (i.e., it is twenty-seven and a half feet deep). For patrons willing to pay more than the general admission charged of the groundlings, there were to be three galleries provided with seats. From the third chief source, stage directions, one learns that entrance to the stage was by doors, presumably spaced widely apart at the rear ("Enter one citizen at one door, and another at the other"), and that in addition to the platform stage there was occasionally some sort of curtained booth or alcove allowing for "discovery" scenes, and some sort of playing space "aloft" or "above" to represent (for example) the top of a city's walls or a room above the street. Doubtless each theater had its own peculiarities, but perhaps we can talk about a "typical" Elizabethan theater if we realize that no theater need exactly have fit the description, just as no father is the typical father with 3.7 children. This hypothetical theater is wooden, round or polygonal (in *Henry V* Shakespeare calls it a "wooden *O*"), capable of holding some eight hundred spectators standing in the yard around the projecting elevated stage and some fifteen hundred additional spectators seated in the three roofed galleries. The stage, protected by a "shadow" or "heavens" or roof, is entered by two doors; behind the doors is the "tiring house" (attiring house, i.e., dressing room), and above the doors is some sort of gallery that may sometimes hold spectators but that can be used (for example) as the bedroom from which Romeo—according to a stage direction in one text—"goeth down." Some evidence suggests that a throne can be lowered onto the platform stage, perhaps from the "shadow"; certainly characters can descend from the stage through a trap or traps into the cellar or "hell." Sometimes this space beneath the platform accommodates a sound-effects man or musician (in *Antony and Cleopatra* "music of the hautboys is under the stage") or an actor (in *Hamlet* the "Ghost cries under the stage"). Most characters simply walk on and off, but because there is no curtain in front of the platform, corpses will have to be carried off (Hamlet must lug Polonius' guts into the neighbor room), or will have to fall at the rear, where the curtain on the alcove or booth can be drawn to conceal them.

Such may have been the so-called "public theater." Another kind of theater, called the "private theater" because its much greater admission charge limited its audience to the wealthy or the prodigal, must be briefly mentioned. The private theater was basically a large room, entirely roofed and therefore artificially illuminated, with a stage at one end. In 1576 one such theater was established in Blackfriars, a Dominican priory in London that had been suppressed in 1538 and confiscated by the Crown and thus was not under the city's jurisdiction. All the actors in the Blackfriars theater were boys about eight to thirteen years old (in the public theaters similar boys played female parts; a boy Lady Macbeth played to a man Macbeth). This private theater had a precarious existence, and ceased operations in 1584. In 1596 James Burbage, who had already made theatrical history by building the Theatre, began to construct a second Blackfriars theater. He died in 1597, and for several years this second Blackfriars theater was used by a troupe of boys, but in 1608 two of Burbage's sons and five other actors (including Shakespeare) became joint operators of the theater, using it in the winter when the open-air Globe was unsuitable. Perhaps such a smaller theater, roofed, artificially illuminated, and with a tradition of a courtly audience, exerted an influence on Shakespeare's late plays.

Performances in the private theaters may well have had intermissions during which music was played, but in the public theaters the action was probably uninterrupted, flowing from scene to scene almost without a break. Actors would enter, speak, exit, and others would immediately enter and establish (if necessary) the new locale by a few properties and by words and gestures. Here are some samples of Shakespeare's scene painting:

> This is Illyria, lady.

> Well, this is the Forest of Arden.

> This castle hath a pleasant seat; the air
> Nimbly and sweetly recommends itself
> Unto our gentle senses.

On the other hand, it is a mistake to conceive of the Elizabethan stage as bare. Although Shakespeare's Chorus in *Henry V* calls the stage an "unworthy scaffold" and urges the spectators to "eke out our performance with your mind," there was considerable spectacle. The last act of *Macbeth,* for example, has five stage directions calling for "drum and colors," and another sort of appeal to the eye is indicated by the stage direction "Enter Macduff, with Macbeth's head." Some scenery and properties may have been substantial; doubtless a throne was used, and in one play of the period we encounter this direction: "Hector takes up a great piece of rock and casts at Ajax, who tears up a young tree by the roots and assails Hector." The matter is of some importance, and will be glanced at again in the next section.

The Texts of Shakespeare

Though eighteen of his plays were published during his lifetime, Shakespeare seems never to have supervised their publication. There is nothing unusual here; when a playwright sold a play to a theatrical company he surrendered his ownership of it. Normally a company would not publish the play, because to publish it meant to allow competitors to acquire the piece. Some plays, however, did get published: apparently treacherous actors sometimes pieced together a play for a publisher, sometimes a company in need of money sold a play, and sometimes a company allowed a play to be published that no longer drew audiences. That Shakespeare did not concern himself with publication, then, is scarcely remarkable; of his contemporaries only Ben Jonson carefully supervised the publication of his own plays. In 1623, seven years after Shakespeare's death, John Heminges and Henry Condell (two senior members of Shakespeare's company, who had performed with him for about twenty years) collected his plays—published and unpublished—into a large volume, commonly called the First Folio. (A folio is a volume consisting of sheets that have been folded once, each sheet thus making two leaves, or four pages. The eighteen plays published during Shakespeare's lifetime had been issued one play per volume in small books called quartos. Each sheet in a quarto has been folded twice, making four leaves, or eight pages.) The First Folio contains thirty-six plays; a thirty-seventh, *Pericles,* though not in the Folio is regarded as canonical. Heminges and Condell suggest in an address "To the great variety of readers" that the republished plays are presented in better form than in the quartos: "Before you were abused with diverse stolen and surreptitious copies, maimed and deformed by the frauds and stealths of injurious impostors that exposed them; even those, are now offered to your view cured and perfect of their limbs, and all the rest absolute in their numbers, as he [i.e., Shakespeare] conceived them."

Whoever was assigned to prepare the texts for publication in the First Folio seems to have taken his job seriously and yet not to have performed it with uniform care. The sources of the texts seem to have been, in general, good unpublished copies or the best published copies. The first play in the collection, *The Tempest,* is divided into acts and scenes, has unusually full stage directions and descriptions of spectacle, and concludes with a list of the characters, but the editor was not able (or willing) to present all of the succeeding texts so fully dressed. Later texts occasionally show signs of carelessness: in one scene of *Much Ado About Nothing* the names of actors, instead of characters, appear as speech prefixes, as they had in the quarto, which the Folio reprints; proofreading throughout the Folio is spotty and apparently was done without reference to the printer's copy; the pagination of *Hamlet* jumps from 156 to 257.

A modern editor of Shakespeare must first select his copy; no problem if the play exists only in the Folio, but a considerable problem if the relationship between a quarto and the Folio—or an early quarto and a later one—is unclear. When an editor has chosen what seems to him to be the most authoritative text or texts for his copy, he has not done with making decisions. First of all, he must reckon with Elizabethan spelling. If he is not producing a facsimile, he probably modernizes it, but ought he to preserve the old form of words that apparently were pronounced quite unlike their modern forms—"lanthorn," "alablaster"? If he preserves these forms, is he really preserving Shakespeare's forms or perhaps those of a compositor in the printing house? What is one to do when one finds "lanthorn" and "lantern" in adjacent lines? (The editors of this series in general, but not invariably, assume that words should be spelled in their modern form.) Elizabethan punctuation, too, presents problems. For example in the First Folio, the only text for the play, Macbeth rejects his wife's idea that he can wash the blood from his hand:

> no: this my Hand will rather
> The multitudinous Seas incarnardine,
> Making the Greene one, Red.

Obviously an editor will remove the superfluous capitals, and he will probably alter the spelling to "incarnadine," but will he leave the comma before "red," letting Macbeth speak of the sea as "the green one," or will he (like most modern editors) remove the comma and thus have Macbeth say that his hand will make the ocean *uniformly* red?

An editor will sometimes have to change more than spelling or punctuation. Macbeth says to his wife:

> I dare do all that may become a man,
> Who dares no more, is none.

For two centuries editors have agreed that the second line is unsatisfactory, and have emended "no" to "do": "Who dares do more is none." But when in the same play Ross says that fearful persons

> floate vpon a wilde and violent Sea
> Each way, and moue,

need "move" be emended to "none," as it often is, on the hunch that the compositor misread the manuscript? The editors of the Signet Classic Shakespeare have restrained themselves from making abundant emendations. In their minds they hear Dr. Johnson on the dangers of emending: "I have adopted the Roman sentiment, that it is more honorable to save a citizen than to kill an enemy." Some departures (in addition to spelling, punctuation, and lineation) from the copy text have of course been made, but the original readings are listed in a note following the play, so that the reader can evaluate them for himself.

The editors of the Signet Classic Shakespeare, following tradition, have added line numbers and in many cases act and scene divisions as well as indications of locale at the beginning of scenes. The Folio divided most of the plays into acts and some into scenes. Early eighteenth-century editors increased the divisions. These divisions, which provide a convenient way of referring to passages in the plays, have been retained, but when not in the text chosen as the basis for the Signet Classic text they are enclosed in square brackets [ ] to indicate that they are editorial additions. Similarly, although no play of Shakespeare's published during his lifetime was equipped with indications of locale at the heads of scene divisions, locales have here been added in square brackets for the convenience of the reader, who lacks the information afforded to spectators by costumes, properties, and gestures. The spectator can tell at a glance he is in the throne room, but without an editorial indication the reader may be puzzled for a while. It should be mentioned, incidentally, that there are a few authentic stage directions —perhaps Shakespeare's, perhaps a prompter's—that suggest locales: for example, "Enter Brutus in his orchard," and "They go up into the Senate house." It is hoped that the bracketed additions provide the reader with the sort of help provided in these two authentic directions, but it is equally hoped that the reader will remember that the stage was not loaded with scenery.

No editor during the course of his work can fail to recollect some words Heminges and Condell prefixed to the Folio:

It had been a thing, we confess, worthy to have been wished, that the author himself had lived to have set forth and overseen his own writings. But since it hath been ordained otherwise, and he by death departed from that right, we pray you do not envy his friends the office of their care and pain to have collected and published them.

Nor can an editor, after he has done his best, forget Heminges and Condell's final words: "And so we leave you to other of his friends, whom if you need can be your guides. If you need them not, you can lead yourselves, and others. And such readers we wish him."

SYLVAN BARNET
Tufts University

Introduction

Perhaps more than any other work of Shakespeare's, *The Two Gentlemen of Verona* needs to be taken for what it is: a product of its time written by a young poet-dramatist seeking his way in what was for him a new genre. So understood, it requires no defense and no apology.

The genre was romantic comedy, in the sense we mean when we mention the masterpieces that would follow in quick succession—*The Merchant of Venice, Much Ado About Nothing, As You Like It,* and *Twelfth Night.* The date of *The Two Gentlemen of Verona* is uncertain; the play may have been written as early as 1590–91, or as late as 1594–95. Most likely it was written in about 1592–93. But however late or early, within these extremes, it was for Shakespeare the first of a kind. Probably the only comedy he had written before it was *The Comedy of Errors,* a generally more satisfactory work than this, but one of an essentially different species, which gave him little practice toward the new kind that he was attempting. For the *Errors* he had a model, a good one, made by a master craftsman of Latin comedy, Plautus. Though Shakespeare injected certain romantic elements into this model, or grafted them onto it, the finished work remained rather more Plautine than Shakespearean, more a succession of farcical incidents than a pattern woven of romance elements.

And in the unlikely event that *The Two Gentlemen of Verona* followed rather than preceded *Love's Labor's*

Lost[1] and *The Taming of the Shrew,* it must yet be said that Shakespeare gained from these very little practice toward his new genre. *Love's Labor's Lost* was aimed satirically at fashionable but outlandish excesses in courtly language, manners, and ideas, and to the exploitation of these excesses the elements of romance were only incidental. The main plot of the *Shrew,* that of the taming, had no place at all for romance, in either atmosphere or action; it was hilarious farce, done in burlesque proportions. Nor did the secondary plot, that of the competition for Bianca, offer happy accommodation to the spirit and mood of romance; it turned upon a game of "supposes," in which only the attitudes of farce could be at home.

Whether before or after *Love's Labor's Lost* and *The Taming of the Shrew,* then, it was with *The Two Gentlemen of Verona* that Shakespeare found the way that led to the ultimate *Twelfth Night.* The basic stuff of romance, of course, lay around him everywhere, in prose and verse, in English, French, Spanish, and Italian, in medieval and in contemporary tellings and retellings. Long before *The Two Gentlemen of Verona* was written, the materials of romance had grown enamored of specific themes and encrusted with specific conventions. The theme of conflict between friendship and love was one that Chaucer had used and that was used again and again, in various forms of romantic tale and in various countries; indeed, Shakespeare's own sonnets play variations upon this theme, in the shadowy outline of a story that they tell of friendship between young men, of jealousy and separation occasioned by love of a third person, and finally of reconciliation. Lyly in his *Euphues,* Sidney in his *Arcadia,* less well-known contemporary romancers and translators all contributed to make the matters of romance, their themes and conventions, familiar to everyone who read or listened, familiar enough, indeed, that in any

---

[1] For an argument to the contrary, suggesting that *Love's Labors Lost* may be as early as 1588, see Alfred Harbage, "*Love's Labor's Lost* and the Early Shakespeare," *Philological Quarterly,* XLI (1962), 18–36.

"new" romance, how a friend or lover, hero or heroine would behave in a given situation might be foretold with considerable accuracy.

What Shakespeare undertook in *The Two Gentlemen of Verona* was the experimental task of adapting the materials, themes, and conventions of meandering narrative romance (or of lyric verse) to dramatic form— to create action that might be contained in two hours, characters sufficiently credible that they might be represented by corporeal actors on a stage, a "world" of sufficient density to sustain both the action and the characters. For what he attempted there was nothing like a satisfactory precedent. For *The Comedy of Errors* he had had Plautus' *Menaechmi;* for the new genre of romantic comedy, he had nothing more suitable than, say, Lyly's *Endimion,* which was useful in every way except the one way that was needed; instead of being dramatically solid, *Endimion* was as watery as the moon.

For his principal story he turned to the tale of her life told by the shepherdess Felismena, in the *Diana Enamorada* of Jorge de Montemayor, of which the relevant portions are reprinted after the text in this edition of the play. But in fact the whole reservoir of romance served him, inevitably, whether he would or no. Its conventions, intruding, have made three centuries of critics of *The Two Gentlemen* wince: How could Proteus have been so dastardly as to betray, in an instant, his beloved, his friend, and his royal host—not to mention his own honor? How could Valentine so abruptly forgive his disloyal friend all his trespasses? How could he as quickly proffer his beloved Silvia to the miscreant Proteus who only a moment before threatened to rape her? How could Silvia—the daughter of a duke—stand by without a word during this base interchange? How could Julia, after this exhibition of general dastardliness, on the second or third bounce, welcome back her errant lover?

Indeed, very nearly the sole good thing that critics have found it appropriate to say about *The Two Gentlemen of Verona* is that it was a kind of "dry run" for its great successors, anticipating in many of its details the incidents, persons, and relationships the more masterful delineation of which distinguishes the later romantic comedies. It is impossible to do other than concur—in part—with this view of the play as proving ground for the later, greater works; in fact, we have already gone somewhat beyond concurrence by flatly stating that in this play Shakespeare found the way to *Twelfth Night*. That alone should be praise enough, for it allows to *The Two Gentlemen* the same kind and degree of significance that we allow to *Julius Caesar* when we say that in it Shakespeare first worked out the basic pattern of order and relationships that we have in mind when we speak of "Shakespearean" tragedy.

It is appropriate, therefore, that we review some of the ways in which this first of the romantic comedies prepared for those to come. Perhaps it is just to say that in most cases it furnished no more than an artist's preliminary sketches for the fuller, finished portraits of character, incident, and "world" that would come after. But at the same time that we review these, we should consider whether anything contains merit and deserves praise for itself, aside from being a "first."

A good place to begin is with the heroine. Shakespeare did not invent the bright, daring girl of the comedies who, for one reason or another, casts off the outward signs of her sex and personal identity and goes a-masquerading in the world as a man; she existed already in the romances, both in those on which he directly drew for plot and in others which exercised a pervasive influence merely by existing. But in the romances she is a shadowy, pale, and bloodless abstraction that does not come alive enough to be visualized; she would never do on any stage. Shakespeare's creation, in Julia, of the flesh-and-blood heroine who set a great line going was a tremendous achievement. The world of the romantic comedies is a woman's world, and it is dominated by this recurrent figure who masquerades as a man while all of her womanliness is apparent to the audience, which is always aware of her secret. While each belongs to the line, each superlative heroine also has a life that is peculiarly her own. Portia of *The Merchant of Venice,* Rosalind of *As You Like It,* Viola of *Twelfth Night*—these can properly be likened to one another only in the common role they play, in specific recurrent situations in which they take part, and in a kind of brilliance they share that marks them as extraordinary human beings: yet this very brilliance varies markedly in its quality, showing in one as a grand and dignified capability, in another as a mischievous brightness, and in another as a gently feminine and utterly disarming subtlety.

No doubt each of these represents as much of an improvement on Julia as Julia does upon the nebulous female of the prose romances. Nearly every incident in which Julia takes part will be repeated in richer detail by one or more of the later heroines, and just because we are so busy noting the resemblances of the first version to the later ones, and mentally comparing the earlier —to its disadvantage, of course—with the later, we may overlook the peculiar charm of this first heroine herself as she plays her part. Thus in I.ii, Julia's review of the "fair resort of gentlemen" who "every day with parle encounter me" appears a puny forerunner of Portia's review, with Nerissa, of her suitors at Belmont; for one reason, in the latter version Shakespeare knew to give the witty descriptive lines to Portia, not Nerissa, whereas in this first sketch Julia merely asks the questions and it is Lucetta who furnishes the witty replies. But it is in the incident of the letter—an incident that is *not* repeated and thereby shamed by later versions—that we come suddenly upon the fresh and ingratiating charm by which Julia bursts out of the conventions among which the insipid heroines of prose romance move, and comes quite alive; no doubt, this was the first glimpse afforded by the English stage of a new and magnificent creature, the heroine of romantic comedy. The incident immediately follows the review of potential suitors. Lucetta presents a letter from Proteus, and Julia stretches to the tiptoes of indignation in upbraiding her:

> Now, by my modesty, a goodly broker!
> Dare you presume to harbor wanton lines?
> To whisper and conspire against my youth?
> Now, trust me, 'tis an office of great worth,
> And you an officer fit for the place.
> There, take the paper; see it be returned,
> Or else return no more into my sight.
>
> (I.ii.41–47)

This show of spunk is itself worth a good deal; the pale heroine of romance could never have risen to it. Yet the heroine of Shakespearean romantic comedy is not truly born until the next instant, after Lucetta has left the stage; then, thus she speaks:

> And yet I would I had o'erlooked the letter.
> It were a shame to call her back again,
> And pray her to a fault for which I chid her.
> What fool is she, that knows I am a maid,
> And would not force the letter to my view!
>
> (I.ii.50–54)

Shakespeare could definitely have stopped the incident at this; it would have been enough to establish a new institution. But he goes on: Julia calls back Lucetta, takes the letter from her, and, in a simply superb demonstration of the chastity of mind appropriate to highborn ladies in the presence of their lessers, tears it all to bits. Shakespeare could have stopped here, too; it would have been more than enough. But once more he goes on: Lucetta is again dismissed—and in an instant Julia is down on the floor, scrambling to reassemble the pieces:

> Be calm, good wind, blow not a word away
> Till I have found each letter in the letter,
> Except mine own name: that some whirlwind bear
> Unto a ragged, fearful-hanging rock,
> And throw it thence into the raging sea!
>
> (I.ii.118–22)

In later scenes Julia repeatedly breaks the way for her

great successors. In II.vii, she takes the plunge for all of
them: she decides to go to Milan, to check on her—of
course!—completely faithful Proteus; but not in her own
identity:

> Not like a woman, for I would prevent
> The loose encounters of lascivious men.
> Gentle Lucetta, fit me with such weeds
> As may beseem some well-reputed page.
>
> (II.vii.40–43)

This was a fateful step. Soon Portia would say to Nerissa,

> I'll hold thee any wager,
> When we are both accoutred like young men,
> I'll prove the prettier fellow of the two . . .
> (*Merchant of Venice*, III.iv.62–64)

Rosalind would say to Celia,

> Were it not better,
> Because that I am more than common tall,
> That I did suit me all points like a man?
> A gallant curtle-ax upon my thigh,
> A boar-spear in my hand . . .
> (*As You Like It*, I.iii.112–16)

And Viola would say to the Captain, who fished her out
of the deep,

> Conceal me what I am, and be my aid
> For such disguise as haply shall become
> The form of my intent. I'll serve this duke . . .
> (*Twelfth Night*, I.ii.53–55)

The parallels of this kind are numerous. Like all three
of her famed successors, Julia talks with her loved one,
who knows her not. Like Viola, she is sent as an envoy
of love by her truelove to *his* love. Like Portia, she receives from his finger the ring that she gave him. Like
Rosalind, she all but gives away her sex by swooning at a

crucial time. And like all the others, she gets her love at last on terms of uncompromising surrender:

> What is in Silvia's face, but I may spy
> More fresh in Julia's with a constant eye?
> . . . .
> Bear witness, Heaven, I have my wish forever.
> (V.iv.114–15, 119)

In every parallel incident, she suffers from the inevitable comparison, and it is only in the rare moments when we catch her, so to speak, alone, doing something uniquely hers, not "trying out" something that her successors would perfect, that she has a chance to shine. So she does in the incident of the letter, and so, for example, she does in IV.ii, when, wearing boy's clothes and accompanied by the Host, she eavesdrops on Proteus' serenade of Silvia. Here, though the song is all Silvia's, the dramatic center is all Julia's:

Host. How do you, man? The music likes you not.

Julia. You mistake; the musician likes me not.

Host. Why, my pretty youth?

Julia. He plays false, father.

(IV.ii.54–57)

She is great here not merely for the emotional impact of her moment of heartbreak, but for her resilience. The pallid heroine of prose romance would have crawled away to bleed in secret; but Julia asks of the Host, "Where lies Sir Proteus?" Her mind has already conceived a device by which she can keep an eye on him until such time as she can capture him for once and all.

It is almost certain that Proteus and Valentine suffer less by comparison with their successors than does Julia. This will appear a startling statement, particularly with reference to Proteus, who has a long and virtually undeviating history of being abominated by critics. It is nevertheless essentially true, and the reason it is so is not hard to find. The fact is that the heroes of the romantic comedies—unlike the heroines, whose power to dazzle the eye and the imagination makes a beginning with Julia and at once thereafter becomes blinding—never do come to amount to very much. Proteus and Valentine, therefore, look about as good as any.

Between them, these two gentlemen define both of the emphases of which the one or the other dominates the later heroes. It is not strictly accurate to classify Shakespeare's romantic young males in two "types"—one wicked, the other stupid—but it is fair to say that each of them evinces a *tendency* in one or the other direction, and that two of them even tend toward both directions at the same time. To say that they exhibit a tendency toward wickedness or toward stupidity is not to say that they are wicked or stupid, but is to suggest that if they went somewhat farther along the road their qualities point them in, they would indeed be downright wicked or downright stupid. It should be added at once that though this view of the heroes is hardly flattering, surely none of us could seriously wish any one of the heroes changed in the slightest; each is perfect for the thing he is, perfect for the particular dramatic "world" of which he is part—and, what is most important, in each case the brilliant heroine loves the fellow either just as he stands or just as she has made him be by the end of the play.

Valentine is the simpler case, in more ways than one, and we should look at him before we deal with Proteus. Valentine looks ahead to the hero who is best represented by Orlando of *As You Like It*. The main thing to be said of this kind of hero is that there is nothing in the least "wrong" with him. He has nothing but virtues—all the virtues that anyone can name, except brilliance. He is kind, brave, loyal, generous, modest, forgiving—anything and everything as you like it; but any passing remark can make him look like a wonderful simpleton in an instant: "I found him under a tree," says Celia of Orlando, "like a dropped acorn." If Valentine is not quite up to Orlando in the kind that he is, he is nevertheless very nearly his equal, both in the sterling qualities of romantic young manhood that his kind of hero stands for and in the lack of intellectual keenness (especially around heroines) that he also stands for. Valentine is the perfect exemplar of friendship; he would never violate friendship even for love —and he is entirely true to his kind when, in the end, without needing to go through the painful process of thinking about it, he cheerfully offers Silvia—for whom he would just as cheerfully die—to Proteus. He could not do otherwise and be what he is; and because Shakespeare has been entirely clear in showing us what he is, it is we who are at fault if we so much as imagine that he should do otherwise. Valentine shares with Orlando, and not particularly with any of Shakespeare's other heroes of romantic comedy, a certain exaggeratedly heroic valor. Orlando hurls a professional wrestler to the ground, breaking his bones, and deals just as directly, and with no sweat, with a "sucked and hungry" lioness. But he best sums up all the qualities of his kind of romantic hero in a single incident and a single posture when, seeking food for old Adam, he pops into the clearing where the exiled Duke and his followers are at table, and mistaking them all for savages who have never been out of the woods, demands with drawn sword that they "Forbear, and eat no more" until his needs are served. Here, in a stroke, he is heroic on the grand scale, greathearted, nobly unselfish for his old servant—and, quite unconsciously, just a little ludicrous for having so much misjudged the situation.

With such a stroke, Shakespeare imparted a kind of flavor that transformed the romance hero, somewhat as he transformed the vapid romance heroine by adding some special feminine touches, including spunk. Bassanio of *The Merchant of Venice* exhibits the added quality very well when—of all people—he, the golden-fleece hunter, coolly reasons his way past the gold casket and the silver casket and takes the lead one; and he exhibits it again when, in the court scene, after Portia has pinned Shylock to the wall and has him quite at her mercy, he fails to perceive how completely the tables have turned and continues to rush forward, nobly generous, with bags of ducats—Portia's own—to buy off his friend. And this very way of surrounding his hero's grimly stalwart attitude with a tongue-in-cheek attitude Shakespeare first explored in Valentine, notably at his first encounter with the outlaws, upon whom he makes such a favorable impression that they invite him to be "king for our wild faction" after two minutes of conversation. Surely, this is an incident to the abruptness of which critics should take no such exception as some have; like Orlando's heroic-ludicrous posture at the Duke's banquet, and like Valentine's own quick offer to surrender Silvia to Proteus, and like Bassanio's straight-faced choice of the leaden casket, it hints of what Shakespeare did to romance to make it romantic *comedy*.

Thus the attitude of comedy within which the actions of the Valentine-Orlando kind of hero are framed is not limited to the more obvious situations in which the comic potentialities of the hero's intellectual equipment are exploited—as in the case of Valentine's penning a love note for Silvia and not understanding, while the simple Speed is appalled by his obtuseness, that her "secret nameless friend" is himself—but extends to his most heroic and high-minded moments. On both counts, Valentine is more nearly a finished portrait than a first sketch.

At least as much may be said of Proteus, first of those who represent a contrary emphasis in the heroic character. Valentine, Bassanio, Orlando are innocent and goodhearted; none of them could ever be imagined as "going bad" under any circumstances. Proteus not only could but temporarily does go bad, and so do those who follow in his line, namely, Claudio of *Much Ado About Nothing* and—stepping just over the boundary into the "dark comedies"—Bertram of *All's Well That Ends Well*.

These heroes are clearly not so much like one another as are those of the other line, who might almost be said to be interchangeable. Claudio, in particular, shares with the Valentine-Orlando hero a certain congenital unawareness of situation; but, curiously, while this appears a lovable fault in the others and endears them to us as well as to the heroines, in Claudio it is odious. A callow princox of a youth, Claudio looks from the outset like one who could mistake a situation and become nasty about it, as indeed he does. If he is "cured" in the end, when the truth of the situation has been made apparent, yet he remains the same callow princox still, and one supposes that he would be capable of dastardly conduct again tomorrow or the next day if the right set of circumstances invited him. Bertram and Claudio differ most notably in that, while each is capable of dastardly conduct, Claudio's worst exhibition of contemptible qualities is based on his initial misunderstanding of situation, whereas Bertram's involvement in such unheroic activities as illicit pursuits and outright lying is quite deliberate. If Claudio is capable of contemptible behavior only when he misunderstands, Bertram is most capable of it when he understands very well.

As a hero of his kind, therefore, not being in competition with the Valentine-Orlando kind, but compared with Claudio and Bertram, Proteus looks remarkably good. As a dramatic character he is certainly as well drawn as they are, and as a man he is hardly worse than they. Proteus is like Bertram in needing no misunderstanding of situation to start him on a wayward course. It has been remarked of Macbeth that of all Shakespeare's tragic heroes he alone knowingly embraces evil as his good, and it may as well be said of Proteus and Bertram that they alone of the comic heroes knowingly take to the crooked paths of dishonor. Bertram rejects the wife of inferior birth who was forced on him; lies to her; pursues, with the intention of corrupting, for no reason but lust, a virgin of Florence; is prevented from committing adultery only by his wife's shrewd intervention; and thereafter, confronted with his deeds, lies, slanders others, and abandons all dignity and honor in an exhibition of squirming and twisting; and after his disgraceful wallowing, he is abruptly forgiven all his trespasses and welcomed home as a worthy subject, son, and husband.

Against Bertram's record as a hero, Proteus' fairly shines. He does not choose to leave his Julia, but is sent away by his father. Neither does he choose to fall in love with Silvia, any more than Romeo chooses to fall in love with Juliet (and many details of the play prove that Shakespeare had Brooke's *Romeus and Juliet* in mind as he wrote). Here, in reducing the odium of Proteus' initial fault, Shakespeare has been characteristically shrewd, for he has made Silvia irresistible, with both an inward and an outward beauty. If, lest she put Julia in the shade, he had made her only an ordinary beauty, Proteus' "three-fold perjury" committed in pursuit of her would have been difficult to understand and all but impossible to forgive. But on Silvia he has lavished all his superlatives, made her dazzling, wholly worthy of the song with which she is serenaded in Act IV and which is itself incomparable. All things considered, Silvia being as she is and what she is, who can blame Proteus?

In two other ways, also, Shakespeare goes farther toward explaining and extenuating Proteus' fault than he was to do with the faults of Claudio and Bertram. In the first scene of the play, Proteus is shown to be both a faithful friend and a faithful lover; but also the point is made evident that in a crisis of conflict between friendship and love, love would claim him:

> He after honor hunts, I after love.
> He leaves his friends to dignify them more,
> I leave myself, my friends, and all, for love.
>
> (I.i.63–65)

He is love's votary; as it has been with Julia, so will it be with Silvia when the time comes: he will leave himself, his true friend, and all else, for love. Second, as he does not do for Claudio and Bertram, Shakespeare does Proteus the credit of allowing him to debate the right and wrong of his multiple perjury before he commits it, to debate the question, in fact, twice, in II.iv. 191–213, and in II.vi. 1–43. Claudio and Bertram, one notes, engage in no self-debate; they directly announce their bad intentions without troubling with any such preliminaries. Even though his decision is "wrong," Proteus at least undergoes the formality of weighing right and wrong. It is true that his self-debate involves no agonizing soul struggle such as

Angelo of *Measure for Measure* undergoes in a roughly comparable situation, when flesh and the spirit are at war in him; Shakespeare quite rightly keeps Proteus' "struggle" light, superficial, artificial, well within the tone and the terms appropriate to romantic comedy:

> And ev'n that pow'r which gave me first my oath
> Provokes me to this threefold perjury:
> Love bade me swear, and Love bids me forswear.
>
> (II.vi.4–6)

Surely, this is as far as a proper hero of romantic comedy dare go in soul struggle, and critics who deplore the too-easy entrance of Proteus into treachery—even as they deplore his too-easy return from it—would do well to remember that the moral ponderings of a Hamlet, an Angelo, or a Macbeth at this point would crash out of and destroy the very genre that this particular romantic hero helped to create.

But all this is not to suggest that Proteus is a blameless hero; if he were so, he would not belong with Claudio and Bertram, but with Valentine and Orlando. It is rather to insist that of the specific kind he represents, he runs true to form and measures up extremely well. Launce identifies him and his kind clearly enough: "I am but a fool, look you, and yet I have the wit to think my master is a kind of a knave." Is he any worse than that? For only a moment he seems to be, when he threatens Silvia with violence in the forest, and here perhaps Shakespeare did indeed go too far. But whether he would actually attack Silvia we neither know nor need to know; the fact is that he does not attack her, and we are quite aware that, with Valentine at hand, watching every move, there never was any real danger in the situation. He is guilty of nothing more than a thoroughly wicked intent, which is thwarted while it is only an impulse. A wicked impulse is not punishable, and in the world of romantic comedy is not even to be thought on too seriously.

Julia and Silvia, Valentine and Proteus are the most notable human fixtures in the special world of romantic comedy that was born with *The Two Gentlemen of Verona*. They are light but durable fixtures, as that world requires. If they are not wholly credible, yet they are more credible than were their forbears in the romances, and they are credible enough, palpable enough, one may say, for the world of romantic comedy, the nature of which would be altered if it were made to sustain creatures more solid. They are of a kind with this special world.

The world of romantic comedy, both as it was first drawn in this play and as it was re-created in each of the masterpieces that followed, of course includes other features besides the heroes and the heroines who invariably inhabit it. It includes, for example, clowns and fools. Speed and Launce stand rather uncertainly between the twin Dromios, the bewildered but witty slaves of *The Comedy of Errors,* before them, and the magnificent creations that came after, like Launcelot Gobbo of *The Merchant of Venice* and Touchstone of *As You Like It*. They are not as gifted as these—if Launcelot Gobbo, a great dunce, may be said to be gifted—and they talk too long with one another and with their masters. With the exception of Launce's long exhortation to his dog to be a better dog, their appearances are likely to be found tedious in both the theater and the study. But if they are not at all well and functionally fitted into the plot of the play— and the fact is that they are almost always purely interruptive—yet Shakespeare's introduction of them into romance helped to bring romantic comedy into being: the oozy world of romance needed their dryness. Their presence does not particularly help to make this incredible world more credible; but it does what is just as good— namely, helps to make the point that this world does not *have* to be perfectly credible, helps to render its very incredibility acceptable. In such a world as they inhabit, how can we reasonably balk at such a turn as the sudden redemption of Proteus or Valentine's magnanimous offer of Silvia? They are reminders that we are to keep our perspective and not consider things too seriously; annoying as they have proved for many critics, with their dreary stretches of low-grade quibbles and mental horseplay, they nevertheless serve the important perspective-giving function implied by Feste's refrain at the end of *Twelfth Night:* ". . . the rain it raineth every day."

Like the heroes and the heroines, the clowns and fools, and the incidents that take extravagant turns, the dramatic verse of *The Two Gentlemen of Verona* needs also to be taken for what it is and does within the world of romantic comedy. No passages and almost no single lines in this play (setting aside the whole of the song to Silvia) are particularly memorable. If one sets, for instance, the poetic language of Julia's interviews (in disguise) with Proteus and with Silvia beside that of Viola-Cesario's interviews with Orsino and Olivia in *Twelfth Night*—a fair comparison, involving similar characters in virtually identical situations—the contrast is obvious enough; yet it is not shocking. Here is Julia-Sebastian speaking to Silvia:

> She hath been fairer, madam, than she is.
> When she did think my master loved her well,
> She, in my judgment, was as fair as you.
> But since she did neglect her looking glass,
> And threw her sun-expelling mask away,
> The air hath starved the roses in her cheeks
> And pinched the lily-tincture of her face,
> That now she is become as black as I.
>
> (IV.iv.149–56)

And here is Viola-Cesario, telling how she-he would woo Olivia:

> Make me a willow cabin at your gate,
> And call upon my soul within the house;
> Write loyal cantons of contemnèd love
> And sing them loud even in the dead of night;
> Halloo your name to the reverberate hills
> And make the babbling gossip of the air
> Cry out "Olivia!"
>
> (*Twelfth Night* I.v.254–60)

There is a resonance, a throaty vibrance in the music of the great poetic passages of *Twelfth Night*—

She never told her love,
But let concealment, like a worm i' th' bud,
Feed on her damask cheek. She pined in thought,
And with a green and yellow melancholy
She sat, like Patience on a monument,
Smiling at grief.

(II.iv.109–14)

—to which at best *The Two Gentlemen of Verona* never once attains, unless in the single line so much praised by Logan Pearsall Smith (*Shakespeare*, p. 74): ". . . but it is only in the *Two Gentlemen of Verona,* with the song 'Who is Silvia,' with the line:

The uncertain glory of an April day,

and the passage about the brook that makes sweet music as it strays, that his power over words becomes a magic power, and his golden mastery of speech begins to almost blind us with its beauty."

Though it is easy to assent to the glory of this single line, no one would be likely to claim particular distinction for all the poetry of the play. What is here asserted, instead, is that the poetic language is "right" for the play, that it helps in the same way that the heroes and heroines and the extravagant incidents do to create the "world" of romantic comedy. This poetry has a good deal of chaff in it; it is sometimes glittering chaff, but chaff it is. It is light and usually frivolous; even when deep ideas are asserted, they are not asserted profoundly. The speakers habitually play along the surface of things:

Proteus. So, by your circumstance, you call me fool.

Valentine. So, by your circumstance, I fear you'll prove.

Proteus. 'Tis love you cavil at. I am not Love.

Valentine. Love is your master, for he masters you;
And he that is so yokèd by a fool,
Methinks, should not be chronicled for wise.

Proteus. Yet writers say, as in the sweetest bud
  The eating canker dwells, so eating love
  Inhabits in the finest wits of all.

Valentine. And writers say . . .

                                                    (I.i.36–45)

This is as typical an example as any of the poetic talk that fills the play, and in filling it defines its kind. It is both superficial and artificial, if one will, but "right" for the kind of world in which it is spoken and which it creates in being spoken, just as, for the same reason, the principal characters and incidents are also "right." There is an attitude of frivolity about this world which is figured forth in language, character, and incident.

Viewed thus, for what it is in part and whole, the play needs no apology, and certainly it does not deserve the harsh criticism that it has received from many who have not been content to take it for what it is. It transformed romance to romantic comedy, and it founded a great line. But, viewed as we have viewed it, it need not depend for its whole credit upon the fact that it was an important "first." It would be what it is if there were no *Twelfth Night*—indeed, it would no doubt look much better if there were no *Twelfth Night*.

BERTRAND EVANS
University of California
Berkeley

The
Two Gentlemen
of Verona

The Names of All the Actors

Duke [of Milan], father to Silvia
Valentine ⎱
Proteus ⎰ the two gentlemen
Antonio, father to Proteus
Thurio, a foolish rival to Valentine
Eglamour, agent for Silvia in her escape
Host, where Julia lodges
Outlaws, with Valentine
Speed, a clownish servant to Valentine
Launce, the like to Proteus
Panthino, servant to Antonio
Julia, beloved of Proteus
Silvia, beloved of Valentine
Lucetta, waiting woman to Julia
[Servants, Musicians

Scene: Verona; Milan; a forest]

The Two Gentlemen of Verona

ACT I

Scene I. [*Verona. An open place.*]

[Enter] Valentine [and] Proteus.

Valentine. Cease to persuade, my loving Proteus:
Home-keeping youth have ever homely wits.
Were't not affection chains thy tender days
To the sweet glances of thy honored love,
I rather would entreat thy company   5
To see the wonders of the world abroad,
Than, living dully sluggardized at home,
Wear out thy youth with shapeless idleness.
But since thou lov'st, love still, and thrive therein,
Even as I would, when I to love begin.   10

Proteus. Wilt thou be gone? Sweet Valentine, adieu!
Think on thy Proteus when thou haply°1 seest
Some rare noteworthy object in thy travel:
Wish me partaker in thy happiness
When thou dost meet good hap;° and in thy danger,   15

---

[1] The degree sign (°) indicates a footnote, which is keyed to the
text by line number. Text references are printed in *italic* type;
the annotation follows in roman type.

I.i.12 *haply* by chance   15 *hap* luck

If ever danger do environ thee,
Commend thy grievance to my holy prayers,
For I will be thy beadsman,° Valentine.

Valentine. And on a love-book° pray for my success?

20   *Proteus.* Upon some book I love I'll pray for thee.

Valentine. That's on some shallow story of deep love:
How young Leander° crossed the Hellespont.

Proteus. That's a deep story of a deeper love,
For he was more than over shoes in love.

25   *Valentine.* 'Tis true, for you are over boots in love,
And yet you never swum the Hellespont.

Proteus. Over the boots? Nay, give me not the boots.°

Valentine. No, I will not, for it boots° thee not.

Proteus.   What?

Valentine. To be in love—where scorn is bought with
     groans,
Coy looks with heartsore sighs, one fading mo-
30   ment's mirth
With twenty watchful, weary, tedious nights;
If haply won, perhaps a hapless° gain;
If lost, why then a grievous labor won;
However,° but a folly bought with wit,
35   Or else a wit by folly vanquishèd.

Proteus. So, by your circumstance,° you call me fool.

Valentine. So, by your circumstance, I fear you'll
prove.

Proteus. 'Tis love you cavil at. I am not Love.

Valentine. Love is your master, for he masters you;

18 *beadsman* one who contracts to pray in behalf of another   19
love-book i.e., instead of a prayer book   22 *Leander* (legendary
Greek youth who nightly swam the Hellespont to visit his beloved
Hero and, one night, was drowned)   27 *give me not the boots* i.e.,
don't jest with me   28 *boots* benefits (with pun on preceding line)
32 *hapless* luckless   34 *However* in either case   36 *by your circumstance* i.e., by your argument (in the next line the same phrase
means "in your condition [of love]")

And he that is so yokèd by a fool,   40
Methinks, should not be chronicled° for wise.

Proteus. Yet writers say, as in the sweetest bud
The eating canker° dwells, so eating love
Inhabits in the finest wits of all.

Valentine. And writers say, as the most forward° bud   45
Is eaten by the canker ere it blow,°
Even so by love the young and tender wit
Is turned to folly, blasting° in the bud,
Losing his verdure even in the prime,°
And all the fair effects of future hopes.   50
But wherefore waste I time to counsel thee,
That art a votary to fond desire?
Once more adieu! My father at the road°
Expects my coming, there to see me shipped.

Proteus. And thither will I bring° thee, Valentine.   55

Valentine. Sweet Proteus, no; now let us take our
    leave.
To Milan let me hear from thee by letters
Of thy success° in love, and what news else
Betideth here in absence of thy friend,
And I likewise will visit thee with mine.   60

Proteus. All happiness bechance to thee in Milan!

Valentine. As much to you at home! And so, farewell.
                                                    Exit.

Proteus. He after honor hunts, I after love.
He leaves his friends to dignify them more,
I leave myself, my friends, and all, for love.   65
Thou, Julia, thou hast metamorphized me,
Made me neglect my studies, lose my time,
War with good counsel, set the world at nought,
Made wit with musing weak, heart sick with
    thought.

___

41 *chronicled* written down   43 *canker* cankerworm   45 *most forward* earliest   46 *blow* bloom   48 *blasting* withering   49 *prime*
spring   53 *road* harbor   55 *bring* accompany   58 *success* fortune
(good or bad)

[*Enter Speed.*]

70 *Speed.* Sir Proteus, save you!° Saw you my master?

Proteus. But now he parted hence, to embark for
Milan.

Speed. Twenty to one, then, he is shipped already,
And I have played the sheep° in losing him.

Proteus. Indeed, a sheep doth very often stray,
75 And if° the shepherd be awhile away.

Speed. You conclude that my master is a shepherd,
then, and I a sheep?

Proteus. I do.

Speed. Why then, my horns are his horns,° whether I
80 wake or sleep.

Proteus. A silly answer, and fitting well a sheep.

Speed. This proves me still a sheep.

Proteus. True, and thy master a shepherd.

Speed. Nay, that I can deny by a circumstance.°

85 *Proteus.* It shall go hard but I'll prove it by another.

Speed. The shepherd seeks the sheep, and not the
sheep the shepherd; but I seek my master, and my
master seeks not me. Therefore I am no sheep.

Proteus. The sheep for fodder follow the shepherd;
90 the shepherd for food follows not the sheep; thou
for wages followest thy master, thy master for
wages follows not thee. Therefore thou art a sheep.

Speed. Such another proof will make me cry "baa."

Proteus. But, dost thou hear? Gav'st thou my letter to
95 Julia?

---

70 *save you* (a greeting)   73 *sheep* (pun on "ship")   75 *And if* if
79 *my horns are his horns* i.e., my (sheep's) horns belong to him
(making him a cuckold)   84 *circumstance* logical proof

Speed. Ay, sir: I, a lost mutton, gave your letter to
her, a laced mutton,° and she, a laced mutton, gave
me, a lost mutton, nothing for my labor.

Proteus. Here's too small a pasture for such store of
muttons.   100

Speed. If the ground be overcharged,° you were best
stick° her.

Proteus. Nay, in that you are astray; 'twere best
pound° you.

Speed. Nay, sir, less than a pound shall serve me for   105
carrying your letter.

Proteus. You mistake. I mean the pound—a pinfold.

Speed. From a pound to a pin? Fold it over and over,
'Tis threefold too little for carrying a letter to your
lover.

Proteus. But what said she?   110

Speed. [*Nodding*] Ay.

Proteus. Nod—ay. Why, that's noddy.°

Speed. You mistook, sir. I say she did nod; and you
ask me if she did nod, and I say, "Ay."

Proteus. And that set together is noddy.   115

Speed. Now you have taken the pains to set it together,
take it for your pains.

Proteus. No, no. You shall have it for bearing the
letter.

Speed. Well, I perceive I must be fain to bear with   120
you.

Proteus. Why, sir, how do you bear with me?

96-97 *lost mutton . . . laced mutton* i.e., lost sheep and laced
courtesan (probably "lost" and "laced" were similarly pronounced)
101 *overcharged* overgrazed   102 *stick* stab (slaughter)   104 *pound*
impound (with pun)   112 *noddy* fool

Speed. Marry,° sir, the letter, very orderly; having
nothing but the word "noddy" for my pains.

125 *Proteus.* Beshrew° me, but you have a quick wit.

Speed. And yet it cannot overtake your slow purse.

Proteus. Come, come, open the matter in brief. What
said she?

Speed. Open your purse, that the money and the mat-
130   ter may be both at once delivered.

Proteus. Well, sir, here is for your pains. What said
she?

Speed. Truly, sir, I think you'll hardly win her.

Proteus. Why, couldst thou perceive so much from
135   her?

Speed. Sir, I could perceive nothing at all from her;
no, not so much as a ducat for delivering your letter.
And being so hard to me that brought your mind,
I fear she'll prove as hard to you in telling your
140   mind. Give her no token but stones;° for she's as
hard as steel.

Proteus. What said she? Nothing?

Speed. No, not so much as "Take this for thy pains."
To testify your bounty, I thank you, you have tes-
145   terned me;° in requital whereof, henceforth carry
your letters yourself. And so, sir, I'll commend you
to my master.

Proteus. Go, go, be gone, to save your ship from wrack,
Which cannot perish, having thee aboard,
150   Being destined to a drier death on shore.°
                                            [*Exit Speed.*]

---

123 *Marry* by the Virgin Mary (a casual oath)   125 *Beshrew* curse
(used casually)   140 *stones* (in addition to punning on its meanings
of "jewels" and "worthless gifts," Speed may be punning on another
meaning, "testicles")   144–45 *testerned me* i.e., given me a testern
(sixpence)   150 *Being destined ... shore* i.e., being destined to hang

I must go send some better messenger;
I fear my Julia would not deign my lines,
Receiving them from such a worthless post.°   *Exit.*

Scene II. [*Verona. Julia's house.*]

Enter Julia and Lucetta.

Julia. But say, Lucetta, now we are alone,
  Wouldst thou, then, counsel me to fall in love?

Lucetta. Ay, madam; so you stumble not unheedfully.

Julia. Of all the fair resort of gentlemen°
  That every day with parle° encounter me,   5
  In thy opinion which is worthiest love?

Lucetta. Please you repeat their names, I'll show my mind
  According to my shallow simple skill.

Julia. What think'st thou of the fair Sir Eglamour?

Lucetta. As of a knight well-spoken, neat, and fine;   10
  But, were I you, he never should be mine.

Julia. What think'st thou of the rich Mercatio?

Lucetta. Well of his wealth; but of himself, so so.

Julia. What think'st thou of the gentle Proteus?

Lucetta. Lord, Lord! To see what folly reigns in us!   15

Julia. How now! What means this passion° at his name?

Lucetta. Pardon, dear madam; 'tis a passing° shame
  That I, unworthy body as I am,
  Should censure° thus on lovely gentlemen.

153 *post* messenger I.ii.4 *resort of gentlemen* crowd of suitors 5
parle parley 16 *passion* emotion 17 *passing* surpassing 19 *censure* pass judgment

20   *Julia.* Why not on Proteus, as of all the rest?

Lucetta. Then thus: of many good I think him best.

Julia. Your reason?

Lucetta. I have no other but a woman's reason:
I think him so because I think him so.

25   *Julia.* And wouldst thou have me cast my love on him?

Lucetta. Ay, if you thought your love not cast away.

Julia. Why, he, of all the rest, hath never moved° me.

Lucetta. Yet he, of all the rest, I think, best loves ye.

Julia. His little speaking shows his love but small.

30   *Lucetta.* Fire that's closest kept burns most of all.

Julia. They do not love that do not show their love.

Lucetta. O, they love least that let men know their love.

Julia. I would I knew his mind.

Lucetta. Peruse this paper, madam.

35   *Julia.* "To Julia."—Say, from whom?

Lucetta. That the contents will show.

Julia. Say, say, who gave it thee?

Lucetta. Sir Valentine's page; and sent, I think, from
Proteus.
He would have given it you; but I, being in the way,
40   Did in your name receive it. Pardon the fault, I pray.

Julia. Now, by my modesty, a goodly broker!°
Dare you presume to harbor wanton lines?
To whisper and conspire against my youth?
Now, trust me, 'tis an office of great worth,
45   And you an officer fit for the place.
There, take the paper; see it be returned,
Or else return no more into my sight.

27 *moved* i.e., proposed to   41 *broker* go-between

Lucetta. To plead for love deserves more fee than hate.

Julia. Will ye be gone?

Lucetta.   That you may ruminate.   *Exit.*

Julia. And yet I would I had o'erlooked° the letter.   50
  It were a shame to call her back again,
  And pray her to° a fault for which I chid her.
  What fool is she, that knows I am a maid,
  And would not force the letter to my view!
  Since maids, in modesty, say "no" to that   55
  Which they would have the profferer construe "ay."
  Fie, fie, how wayward is this foolish love,
  That, like a testy° babe, will scratch the nurse,
  And presently,° all humbled, kiss the rod!
  How churlishly I chid Lucetta hence,   60
  When willingly I would have had her here!
  How angerly I taught my brow to frown,
  When inward joy enforced my heart to smile!
  My penance is to call Lucetta back
  And ask remission for my folly past.   65
  What, ho! Lucetta!

[Enter Lucetta.]

Lucetta.   What would your ladyship?

Julia. Is't near dinnertime?

Lucetta.   I would it were;
  That you might kill your stomach° on your meat,
  And not upon your maid.°

Julia. What is't that you took up so gingerly?   70

Lucetta. Nothing.

Julia. Why didst thou stoop, then?

Lucetta. To take a paper up that I let fall.

---

50 *o'erlooked* perused   52 *pray her to* apologize to her for   58 *testy* irritable   59 *presently* immediately   68 *kill your stomach* (1) allay your vexation (2) appease your hunger   68–69 *meat . . . maid* (pun on "mate")

Julia. And is that paper nothing?

75 *Lucetta.* Nothing concerning me.

Julia. Then let it lie for those that it concerns.

Lucetta. Madam, it will not lie where it concerns,°
Unless it have a false interpreter.

Julia. Some love of yours hath writ to you in rhyme.

80 *Lucetta.* That I might sing it, madam, to a tune.
Give me a note: your ladyship can set.°

Julia. As little by such toys° as may be possible.
Best sing it to the tune of "Light o' love."°

Lucetta. It is too heavy for so light a tune.

85 *Julia.* Heavy! Belike it hath some burden,° then?

Lucetta. Ay, and melodious were it, would you sing it.

Julia. And why not you?

Lucetta.   I cannot reach so high.

Julia. Let's see your song. [*Takes the letter.*] How now,
minion!

Lucetta. Keep tune there still, so you will sing it out:
90   And yet methinks I do not like this tune.

Julia. You do not?

Lucetta.   No, madam; 'tis too sharp.

Julia. You, minion, are too saucy.

Lucetta. Nay, now you are too flat,
And mar the concord with too harsh a descant.°
95   There wanteth but a mean° to fill your song.

Julia. The mean is drowned with your unruly bass.

---

77 *lie where it concerns* i.e., express its content falsely (with
quibble on preceding line)   81 *set* set to music   82 *toys* trifles
83 *Light o' love* a contemporary popular ditty   85 *burden* bass refrain (with pun)   94 *descant* improvised harmony   95 *wanteth but
a mean* lacks a tenor part (Proteus?)

Lucetta. Indeed, I bid the base° for Proteus.

Julia. This babble shall not henceforth trouble me.
    Here is a coil with protestation!°   [*Tears the letter.*]
    Go get you gone, and let the papers lie;   100
    You would be fing'ring them, to anger me.

Lucetta. She makes it strange;° but she would be best
        pleased
    To be so ang'red with another letter.   [*Exit.*]

Julia. Nay, would I were so ang'red with the same!
    O hateful hands, to tear such loving words!   105
    Injurious wasps, to feed on such sweet honey,
    And kill the bees, that yield it, with your stings!
    I'll kiss each several° paper for amends.
    Look, here is writ "kind Julia." Unkind Julia!
    As in revenge of thy ingratitude,   110
    I throw thy name against the bruising stones,
    Trampling contemptuously on thy disdain.
    And here is writ "love-wounded Proteus."
    Poor wounded name! My bosom, as a bed,
    Shall lodge thee, till thy wound be throughly°
        healed;   115
    And thus I search° it with a sovereign kiss.
    But twice or thrice was "Proteus" written down.
    Be calm, good wind, blow not a word away
    Till I have found each letter in the letter,
    Except mine own name: that some whirlwind bear   120
    Unto a ragged, fearful-hanging rock,
    And throw it thence into the raging sea!
    Lo, here in one line is his name twice writ,
    "Poor forlorn Proteus, passionate Proteus,
    To the sweet Julia." That I'll tear away.—   125
    And yet I will not, sith° so prettily
    He couples it to his complaining names.

---

97 *bid the base* (in the game of Prisoner's Base, a challenge to
a test of speed [with pun])   99 *coil with protestation* much ado
made up of lover's protestations   102 *makes it strange* i.e., pre-
tends that it is nothing to her   108 *several* separate   115 *throughly*
thoroughly   116 *search* probe (as in cleaning a wound)   126 *sith*
since

Thus will I fold them one upon another.
Now kiss, embrace, contend, do what you will.

[*Enter Lucetta.*]

130 *Lucetta.* Madam,
Dinner is ready, and your father stays.

Julia. Well, let us go.

Lucetta. What, shall these papers lie like telltales here?

Julia. If you respect them, best to take them up.

135 *Lucetta.* Nay, I was taken up for laying them down;
Yet here they shall not lie, for catching cold.

Julia. I see you have a month's mind° to them.

Lucetta. Ay, madam, you may say what sights you see;
I see things too, although you judge I wink.°

140 *Julia.* Come, come; will't please you go?   *Exeunt.*

Scene III. [*Verona. Antonio's house.*]

Enter Antonio and Panthino.

Antonio. Tell me, Panthino, what sad° talk was that
Wherewith my brother held you in the cloister?

Panthino. 'Twas of his nephew Proteus, your son.

Antonio. Why, what of him?

Panthino.   He wond'red that your lordship
5 Would suffer him to spend his youth at home,
While other men, of slender reputation,°
Put forth their sons to seek preferment out:

---

137 *month's mind* i.e., lasting desire   139 *wink* have my eyes shut,
see nothing   I.iii.1 *sad* serious   6 *slender reputation* unimportant
place

   Some to the wars, to try their fortune there,
   Some to discover islands far away,
   Some to the studious universities.   *10*
   For any, or for all these exercises,
   He said that Proteus your son was meet,°
   And did request me to importune you
   To let him spend his time no more at home,
   Which would be great impeachment° to his age,   *15*
   In having known no travel in his youth.

Antonio. Nor need'st thou much importune me to that
   Whereon this month I have been hammering.°
   I have considered well his loss of time,
   And how he cannot be a perfect man,   *20*
   Not being tried and tutored in the world.
   Experience is by industry achieved,
   And perfected° by the swift course of time.
   Then, tell me, whither were I best to send him?

Panthino. I think your lordship is not ignorant   *25*
   How his companion, youthful Valentine,
   Attends the Emperor° in his royal court.

Antonio. I know it well.

Panthino. 'Twere good, I think, your lordship sent him
      thither.
   There shall he practice tilts and tournaments,   *30*
   Hear sweet discourse, converse with noblemen,
   And be in eye of° every exercise
   Worthy his youth and nobleness of birth.

Antonio. I like thy counsel; well hast thou advised.
   And that thou mayst perceive how well I like it,   *35*
   The execution of it shall make known.
   Even with the speediest expedition°
   I will dispatch him to the Emperor's court.

Panthino. Tomorrow, may it please you, Don Al-
      phonso,

12 *meet* fitted   15 *impeachment* detriment   18 *hammering* i.e., pon-
dering   23 *perfected* (accented on first syllable)   27 *Emperor* i.e.,
Duke (of Milan)   32 *be in eye of* have sight of   37 *expedition*
haste

40 With other gentlemen of good esteem,
Are journeying to salute the Emperor,
And to commend their service to his will.

Antonio. Good company; with them shall Proteus go.
And—in good time! Now will we break with° him.

[*Enter Proteus.*]

45 *Proteus.* Sweet love! Sweet lines! Sweet life!
Here is her hand, the agent of her heart.
Here is her oath for love, her honor's pawn.°
O, that our fathers would applaud our loves,
To seal our happiness with their consents!
50 O heavenly Julia!

Antonio. How now! What letter are you reading there?

Proteus. May't please your lordship, 'tis a word or two
Of commendations° sent from Valentine,
Delivered by a friend that came from him.

55 *Antonio.* Lend me the letter; let me see what news.

Proteus. There is no news, my lord, but that he writes
How happily he lives, how well beloved
And daily gracèd by the Emperor,
Wishing me with him, partner of his fortune.

60 *Antonio.* And how stand you affected to his wish?

Proteus. As one relying on your lordship's will,
And not depending on his friendly wish.

Antonio. My will is something sorted° with his wish.
Muse not that I thus suddenly proceed,
65 For what I will, I will, and there an end.
I am resolved that thou shalt spend some time
With Valentinus in the Emperor's court.
What maintenance he from his friends receives,
Like exhibition° thou shalt have from me.
70 Tomorrow be in readiness to go.

44 *break with* break the news to   47 *pawn* pledge   53 *commendations* greetings   63 *something sorted* somewhat in accord   69 *exhibition* allowance

Excuse it not,° for I am peremptory.°

Proteus. My lord, I cannot be so soon provided.
Please you, deliberate a day or two.

Antonio. Look what° thou want'st shall be sent after
thee.
No more of stay! Tomorrow thou must go.   75
Come on, Panthino; you shall be employed
To hasten on his expedition.

                    [*Exeunt Antonio and Panthino.*]

Proteus. Thus have I shunned the fire for fear of
burning,
And drenched me in the sea, where I am drowned.
I feared to show my father Julia's letter,   80
Lest he should take exceptions to my love;
And with the vantage of mine own excuse
Hath he excepted most against my love.°
O, how this spring of love resembleth
The uncertain glory of an April day,   85
Which now shows all the beauty of the sun,
And by and by a cloud takes all away!

                    [*Enter Panthino.*]

Panthino. Sir Proteus, your father calls for you.
He is in haste; therefore, I pray you, go.

Proteus. Why, this it is: my heart accords thereto,   90
And yet a thousand times it answers "no."   *Exeunt.*

---

71 *Excuse it not* offer no excuses   **71** *peremptory* determined
74 *Look what* whatever   **82–83** *with the vantage . . . my love* i.e., he
took advantage of my own device (the pretended letter from Valentine) to strike the heaviest blow to my affair of love (with Julia)

ACT II

Scene I. [*Milan. The Duke's palace.*]

Enter Valentine [and] Speed.

Speed. Sir, your glove.

Valentine.   Not mine; my gloves are on.

Speed. Why, then, this may be yours, for this is but one.°

Valentine. Ha, let me see. Ay, give it me, it's mine.
Sweet ornament that decks a thing divine!
5   Ah, Silvia, Silvia!

Speed. Madam Silvia! Madam Silvia!

Valentine. How now, sirrah?°

Speed. She is not within hearing, sir.

Valentine. Why, sir, who bade you call her?

10   *Speed.* Your worship, sir, or else I mistook.

Valentine. Well, you'll still° be too forward.

Speed. And yet I was last chidden for being too slow.

Valentine. Go to, sir. Tell me, do you know Madam
Silvia?

II.i.1–2 *on . . . one* (a pun in Elizabethan speech)   7 *sirrah* (common form of address to inferiors)   11 *still* always

58

Speed. She that your worship loves?   15

Valentine. Why, how know you that I am in love?

Speed. Marry, by these special marks: first, you have
learned, like Sir Proteus, to wreathe your arms, like
a malcontent; to relish a love song, like a robin red-
breast; to walk alone, like one that had the pesti-   20
lence; to sigh, like a schoolboy that had lost his
A B C; to weep, like a young wench that had buried
her grandam; to fast, like one that takes diet; to
watch,° like one that fears robbing; to speak puling,°
like a beggar at Hallowmas.° You were wont, when   25
you laughed, to crow like a cock; when you walked,
to walk like one of the lions; when you fasted, it
was presently after dinner; when you looked sadly,
it was for want of money. And now you are metamorphized with a mistress, that,° when I look on   30
you, I can hardly think you my master.

Valentine. Are all these things perceived in me?

Speed. They are all perceived without ye.°

Valentine. Without me? They cannot.

Speed. Without you? Nay, that's certain, for, without°   35
you were so simple, none else would. But you are
so without these follies, that these follies are within
you, and shine through you like the water in an
urinal, that not an eye that sees you but is a physi-
cian to comment on your malady.   40

Valentine. But tell me, dost thou know my lady Silvia?

Speed. She that you gaze on so as she sits at supper?

Valentine. Hast thou observed that? Even she, I mean.

Speed. Why, sir, I know her not.

---

24 *watch* lie awake   24 *puling* whiningly   25 *at Hallowmas* on All
Saints' Day (when beggars vied for special treats)   30 *that* so
that   33 *without ye* i.e., by external signs (here begins a series
of quibbles)   35 *without* unless

45 *Valentine.* Dost thou know her by my gazing on her,
and yet know'st her not?

Speed. Is she not hard-favored,° sir?

Valentine. Not so fair, boy, as well-favored.

Speed. Sir, I know that well enough.

50 *Valentine.* What dost thou know?

Speed. That she is not so fair as, of you, well favored.

Valentine. I mean that her beauty is exquisite, but her
favor° infinite.

Speed. That's because the one is painted, and the other
55 out of all count.°

Valentine. How painted? And how out of count?

Speed. Marry, sir, so painted, to make her fair, that
no man counts of° her beauty.

Valentine. How esteem'st thou me? I account of her
60 beauty.

Speed. You never saw her since she was deformed.°

Valentine. How long hath she been deformed?

Speed. Ever since you loved her.

Valentine. I have loved her ever since I saw her; and
65 still I see her beautiful.

Speed. If you love her, you cannot see her.

Valentine. Why?

Speed. Because Love is blind. O, that you had mine
eyes; or your own eyes had the lights they were wont
70 to have when you chid at Sir Proteus for going
ungartered!°

---

47 *hard-favored* homely   53 *favor* charm, graciousness   55 *out of
all count* beyond counting   58 *counts of* takes account of   61 *deformed* i.e., distorted by your lover's view   70–71 *going ungartered*
(a sure sign that one is in love; see *As You Like It,* III.ii.371)

Valentine. What should I see then?

Speed. Your own present folly, and her passing° de-
formity. For he, being in love, could not see to
garter his hose; and you, being in love, cannot see   75
to put on your hose.

Valentine. Belike, boy, then, you are in love; for last
morning you could not see to wipe my shoes.

Speed. True, sir; I was in love with my bed. I thank
you, you swinged° me for my love, which makes   80
me the bolder to chide you for yours.

Valentine. In conclusion, I stand affected to her.

Speed. I would you were set,° so your affection would
cease.

Valentine. Last night she enjoined me to write some   85
lines to one she loves.

Speed. And have you?

Valentine. I have.

Speed. Are they not lamely writ?

Valentine. No, boy, but as well as I can do them.   90
Peace! Here she comes.

Speed. [*Aside*] O excellent motion! O exceeding puppet! Now will he interpret° to her.

[*Enter Silvia.*]

Valentine. Madam and mistress, a thousand good
morrows.   95

Speed. [*Aside*] O, give ye good ev'n! Here's a million
of manners.

Silvia. Sir Valentine and servant,° to you two thousand.

73 *passing* surpassing, extreme   80 *swinged* beat   83 *set* seated
(quibble on "stand")   92–93 *motion . . . puppet . . . interpret* (the
puppeteer's voice "interprets" for the figures in the puppet play,
or "motion")   98 *servant* gallant lover (i.e., alludes not to Speed
but to Valentine)

Speed. [*Aside*] He should give her interest, and she
100   gives it him.

Valentine. As you enjoined me, I have writ your letter
    Unto the secret nameless friend of yours,
    Which I was much unwilling to proceed in,
    But for my duty to your ladyship.

Silvia. I thank you, gentle servant; 'tis very clerkly°
105   done.

Valentine. Now trust me, madam, it came hardly off;
    For, being ignorant to whom it goes,
    I writ at random, very doubtfully.

Silvia. Perchance you think too much of so much
    pains?

110 *Valentine.* No, madam; so it stead° you, I will write,
    Please you command, a thousand times as much.
    And yet—

Silvia. A pretty period!° Well, I guess the sequel;
    And yet I will not name it; and yet I care not;
115   And yet take this again; and yet I thank you,
    Meaning henceforth to trouble you no more.

Speed. [*Aside*] And yet you will; and yet another "yet."

Valentine. What means your ladyship? Do you not
    like it?

Silvia. Yes, yes: the lines are very quaintly° writ;
120   But since unwillingly, take them again.
    Nay, take them.

Valentine. Madam, they are for you.

Silvia. Ay, ay. You writ them, sir, at my request;
    But I will none of them; they are for you;
125   I would have had them writ more movingly.

Valentine. Please you, I'll write your ladyship another.

Silvia. And when it's writ, for my sake read it over,

105 *clerkly* scholarly   110 *stead* be useful to   113 *period* full stop
119 *quaintly* ingeniously

And if it please you, so; if not, why, so.

Valentine. If it please me, madam, what then?

Silvia. Why, if it please you, take it for your labor;   130
And so, good morrow, servant.   *Exit Silvia.*

Speed. O jest unseen, inscrutable, invisible,
As a nose on a man's face, or a weathercock on a
  steeple!
My master sues to her, and she hath taught her
  suitor,
He being her pupil, to become her tutor.   135
O excellent device! Was there ever heard a better,
That my master, being scribe, to himself should
  write the letter?

Valentine. How now, sir? What are you reasoning with
yourself?

Speed. Nay, I was rhyming; 'tis you that have the   140
reason.

Valentine. To do what?

Speed. To be a spokesman from Madam Silvia.

Valentine. To whom?

Speed. To yourself. Why, she woos you by a figure.°   145

Valentine. What figure?

Speed. By a letter, I should say.

Valentine. Why, she hath not writ to me?

Speed. What need she, when she hath made you write
to yourself? Why, do you not perceive the jest?   150

Valentine. No, believe me.

Speed. No believing you, indeed, sir. But did you
perceive her earnest?°

Valentine. She gave me none, except an angry word.

145 *by a figure* by indirect means   153 *earnest* (1) seriousness
(2) token payment

155 *Speed.* Why, she hath given you a letter.

Valentine. That's the letter I writ to her friend.

Speed. And that letter hath she delivered, and there an end.

Valentine. I would it were no worse.

160 *Speed.* I'll warrant you, 'tis as well;
For often have you writ to her, and she, in modesty,
Or else for want of idle time, could not again reply;
Or fearing else some messenger that might her mind discover,°
Herself hath taught her love himself to write unto her lover.
165 All this I speak in print,° for in print I found it.
Why muse you, sir? 'Tis dinnertime.

Valentine. I have dined.

Speed. Ay, but hearken, sir; though the chameleon Love can feed on the air,° I am one that am nour-
170 ished by my victuals, and would fain have meat. O, be not like your mistress; be moved, be moved.

                                                    Exeunt.

Scene II. [*Verona. Julia's house.*]

Enter Proteus [and] Julia.

Proteus. Have patience, gentle Julia.

Julia. I must, where is no remedy.

Proteus. When possibly I can, I will return.

163 *discover* reveal   165 *speak in print* i.e., quote   168–69 *chameleon . . . the air* (the chameleon was thought to eat nothing but air; see also II.iv.24–26 and *Hamlet* III.ii.95)

Julia. If you turn° not, you will return the sooner.
　Keep this remembrance for thy Julia's sake.　　　　　5
　　　　　　　　　　　　[*Giving a ring.*]

Proteus. Why, then, we'll make exchange; here, take
　you this.

Julia. And seal the bargain with a holy kiss.

Proteus. Here is my hand for my true constancy;
　And when that hour o'erslips me in the day
　Wherein I sigh not, Julia, for thy sake,　　　　　　　10
　The next ensuing hour some foul mischance
　Torment me for my love's forgetfulness!
　My father stays° my coming; answer not;
　The tide is now:—nay, not thy tide of tears;
　That tide will stay me longer than I should.　　　　　15
　Julia, farewell!　　　　　　　　　　[*Exit Julia.*]
　　　　　What, gone without a word?
　Ay, so true love should do: it cannot speak;
　For truth hath better deeds than words to grace it.

[*Enter Panthino.*]

Panthino. Sir Proteus, you are stayed for.

Proteus. Go; I come, I come.　　　　　　　　　　20
　Alas! This parting strikes poor lovers dumb. *Exeunt.*

Scene III. [*Verona. A street.*]

Enter Launce, [leading a dog].

Launce. Nay, 'twill be this hour ere I have done weep-
　ing; all the kind of the Launces have this very fault.
　I have received my proportion,° like the prodigious°

II.ii.4 *turn* i.e., change your affection (perhaps with the additional
meaning of "engage in sexual acts")   13 *stays* waits for   III.iii.3
proportion (Launce's blunder for "portion")   3 *prodigious* (blunder
for "prodigal")

son, and am going with Sir Proteus to the Imperial's
court. I think Crab my dog be the sourest-natured
dog that lives. My mother weeping, my father wailing, my sister crying, our maid howling, our cat
wringing her hands, and all our house in a great
perplexity, yet did not this cruel-hearted cur shed
one tear. He is a stone, a very pebble stone, and
has no more pity in him than a dog. A Jew would
have wept to have seen our parting. Why, my
grandam, having no eyes, look you, wept herself
blind at my parting. Nay, I'll show you the manner
of it. This shoe is my father; no, this left shoe is
my father. No, no, this left shoe is my mother; nay,
that cannot be so neither. Yes, it is so, it is so, it
hath the worser sole. This shoe, with the hole in it,
is my mother, and this my father; a vengeance on't!
There 'tis. Now, sir, this staff is my sister, for, look
you, she is as white as a lily, and as small as a
wand. This hat is Nan, our maid. I am the dog. No,
the dog is himself, and I am the dog. Oh! The dog
is me, and I am myself; ay, so, so. Now come I to
my father: Father, your blessing. Now should not
the shoe speak a word for weeping: now should I
kiss my father: well, he weeps on. Now come I to
my mother. Oh, that she could speak now like a
wood woman!° Well, I kiss her; why, there 'tis.
Here's my mother's breath up and down.° Now
come I to my sister; mark the moan she makes.
Now the dog all this while sheds not a tear, nor
speaks a word; but see how I lay the dust with my
tears.

[*Enter Panthino.*]

Panthino. Launce, away, away, aboard! Thy master is
    shipped, and thou art to post after with oars. What's
    the matter? Why weep'st thou, man? Away, ass!
    You'll lose the tide, if you tarry any longer.

28–29 *Oh, that . . . wood woman* (Launce laments that his [wooden]
shoe is not really his mother, madly distressed [wood] as she was at
parting)   30 *up and down* identically

Launce. It is no matter if the tied were lost; for it is
the unkindest tied that ever any man tied.   40

Panthino. What's the unkindest tide?

Launce. Why, he that's tied here, Crab, my dog.

Panthino. Tut, man, I mean thou'lt lose the flood,°
and, in losing the flood, lose thy voyage, and, in
losing thy voyage, lose thy master, and, in losing   45
thy master, lose thy service, and, in losing thy service— Why dost thou stop my mouth?

Launce. For fear thou shouldst lose thy tongue.

Panthino. Where should I lose my tongue?

Launce. In thy tale.   50

Panthino. In thy tail!

Launce. Lose the tide, and the voyage, and the master,
and the service, and the tied! Why, man, if the river
were dry, I am able to fill it with my tears; if the
wind were down, I could drive the boat with my   55
sighs.

Panthino. Come, come away, man; I was sent to call
thee.

Launce. Sir, call me what thou dar'st.

Panthino. Wilt thou go?   60

Launce. Well, I will go.   *Exeunt.*

Scene IV. [*Milan. The Duke's palace.*]

Enter Valentine, Silvia, Thurio, [and] Speed.

Silvia. Servant!

Valentine. Mistress?

43 *flood* full tide

Speed. Master, Sir Thurio frowns on you.

Valentine. Ay, boy, it's for love.

5 *Speed.* Not of you.

Valentine. Of my mistress, then.

Speed. 'Twere good you knocked him.   [*Exit.*]

Silvia. Servant, you are sad.

Valentine. Indeed, madam, I seem so.

10 *Thurio.* Seem you that you are not?

Valentine. Haply I do.

Thurio. So do counterfeits.

Valentine. So do you.

Thurio. What seem I that I am not?

15 *Valentine.* Wise.

Thurio. What instance of the contrary?

Valentine. Your folly.

Thurio. And how quote° you my folly?

Valentine. I quote it in your jerkin.

20 *Thurio.* My jerkin is a doublet.°

Valentine. Well, then, I'll double your folly.

Thurio. How?

Silvia. What, angry, Sir Thurio! Do you change color?

Valentine. Give him leave, madam; he is a kind of
25   chameleon.

Thurio. That hath more mind to feed on your blood
   than live in your air.

Valentine. You have said, sir.

II.iv.18 *quote* observe (pronounced "coat")   20 *doublet* close-fit-
ting jacket

Thurio. Ay, sir, and done too, for this time.

Valentine. I know it well, sir; you always end ere you   30
begin.

Silvia. A fine volley of words, gentlemen, and quickly
shot off.

Valentine. 'Tis indeed, madam; we thank the giver.

Silvia. Who is that, servant?   35

Valentine. Yourself, sweet lady; for you gave the fire.
Sir Thurio borrows his wit from your ladyship's
looks, and spends what he borrows kindly in your
company.

Thurio. Sir, if you spend word for word with me, I   40
shall make your wit bankrupt.

Valentine. I know it well, sir. You have an exchequer
of words, and, I think, no other treasure to give
your followers, for it appears by their bare° liveries
that they live by your bare words.   45

Silvia. No more, gentlemen, no more—here comes my
father.

[*Enter Duke.*]

Duke. Now, daughter Silvia, you are hard beset.
Sir Valentine, your father's in good health.
What say you to a letter from your friends   50
Of much good news?

Valentine.   My lord, I will be thankful
To any happy messenger° from thence.

Duke. Know ye Don Antonio, your countryman?

Valentine. Ay, my good lord, I know the gentleman
To be of worth, and worthy estimation,   55
And not without desert so well reputed.

Duke. Hath he not a son?

44 *bare* threadbare   52 *happy messenger* i.e., bringer of good news

Valentine. Ay, my good lord, a son that well deserves
The honor and regard of such a father.

60   *Duke.* You know him well?

Valentine. I knew him as myself; for from our infancy
We have conversed and spent our hours together;
And though myself have been an idle truant,
Omitting the sweet benefit of time
65   To clothe mine age with angel-like perfection,
Yet hath Sir Proteus, for that's his name,
Made use and fair advantage of his days;
His years but young, but his experience old;
His head unmellowed, but his judgment ripe.
70   And, in a word, for far behind his worth
Comes all the praises that I now bestow,
He is complete in feature and in mind
With all good grace to grace a gentleman.

Duke. Beshrew me, sir, but if he make this good,
75   He is as worthy for an empress' love
As meet° to be an emperor's counselor.
Well, sir, this gentleman is come to me
With commendation from great potentates,
And here he means to spend his time awhile.
80   I think 'tis no unwelcome news to you.

Valentine. Should I have wished a thing, it had been he.

Duke. Welcome him, then, according to his worth.
Silvia, I speak to you, and you, Sir Thurio;
For Valentine, I need not cite° him to it.
85   I will send him hither to you presently.   [*Exit.*]

Valentine. This is the gentleman I told your ladyship
Had come along with me, but that his mistress
Did hold his eyes locked in her crystal looks.

Silvia. Belike that now she hath enfranchised them,
90   Upon some other pawn for fealty.°

76 *meet* fitted   84 *cite* incite, urge   90 *pawn for fealty* pledge for
loyalty

Valentine. Nay, sure, I think she holds them prisoners
   still.

Silvia. Nay, then, he should be blind; and, being blind,
   How could he see his way to seek out you?

Valentine. Why, lady, Love hath twenty pair of eyes.

Thurio. They say that Love hath not an eye at all.   *95*

Valentine. To see such lovers, Thurio, as yourself.
   Upon a homely object Love can wink. [*Exit Thurio.*]

Silvia. Have done, have done; here comes the gentleman.

[*Enter Proteus.*]

Valentine. Welcome, dear Proteus! Mistress, I beseech
   you,
   Confirm his welcome with some special favor.   *100*

Silvia. His worth is warrant for his welcome hither,
   If this be he you oft have wished to hear from.

Valentine. Mistress, it is. Sweet lady, entertain° him
   To be my fellow servant to your ladyship.

Silvia. Too low a mistress for so high a servant.   *105*

Proteus. Not so, sweet lady, but too mean° a servant
   To have a look of such a worthy mistress.

Valentine. Leave off discourse of disability.°
   Sweet lady, entertain him for your servant.

Proteus. My duty will I boast of, nothing else.   *110*

Silvia. And duty never yet did want his meed.°
   Servant, you are welcome to a worthless mistress.

Proteus. I'll die on° him that says so but yourself.

Silvia. That you are welcome?

103 *entertain* welcome   106 *mean* low, humble   108 *Leave . . . disability* i.e., cease this modest talk   111 *want his meed* lack its re-
ward   113 *die on* fight to the death

Proteus.   That you are worthless.

[*Enter Thurio.*]

Servant. Madam, my lord your father would speak
115   with you.

Silvia. I wait upon his pleasure. [*Exit Servant.*] Come,
Sir Thurio,
Go with me. Once more, new servant, welcome.
I'll leave you to confer of home affairs.
When you have done, we look to hear from you.

120 *Proteus.* We'll both attend upon your ladyship.
[*Exeunt Silvia and Thurio.*]

Valentine. Now, tell me, how do all from whence you
came?

Proteus. Your friends are well, and have them much
commended.°

Valentine. And how do yours?

Proteus.   I left them all in health.

Valentine. How does your lady? And how thrives your
love?

125 *Proteus.* My tales of love were wont to weary you;
I know you joy not in a love discourse.

Valentine. Ay, Proteus, but that life is altered now.
I have done penance for contemning Love,
Whose high imperious thoughts have punished me
130   With bitter fasts, with penitential groans,
With nightly tears, and daily heartsore sighs;
For, in revenge of my contempt of love,
Love hath chased sleep from my enthrallèd eyes,
And made them watchers of mine own heart's sor-
row.
135   O gentle Proteus, Love's a mighty lord,
And hath so humbled me, as° I confess

122 *have them much commended* i.e., themselves to you   136 *as*
that

There is no woe to° his correction,
Nor to his service no such joy on earth.
Now no discourse, except it be of love;
Now can I break my fast, dine, sup, and sleep   *140*
Upon the very naked name of love.

Proteus. Enough; I read your fortune in your eye.
Was this the idol that you worship so?

Valentine. Even she; and is she not a heavenly saint?

Proteus. No; but she is an earthly paragon.   *145*

Valentine. Call her divine.

Proteus.   I will not flatter her.

Valentine. O, flatter me, for love delights in praises.

Proteus. When I was sick, you gave me bitter pills,
And I must minister the like to you.

Valentine. Then speak the truth by her; if not divine, *150*
Yet let her be a principality,
Sovereign to all the creatures on the earth.

Proteus. Except my mistress.

Valentine.   Sweet, except not any,
Except thou wilt except against° my love.

Proteus. Have I not reason to prefer mine own?   *155*

Valentine. And I will help thee to prefer° her too.
She shall be dignified with this high honor—
To bear my lady's train, lest the base earth
Should from her vesture chance to steal a kiss,
And, of so great a favor growing proud,   *160*
Disdain to root the summer-swelling flow'r,
And make rough winter everlastingly.

Proteus. Why, Valentine, what braggardism is this?

Valentine. Pardon me, Proteus. All I can is nothing

---

137 *to* like unto   154 *Except thou wilt except against* unless you
will take exception to   156 *prefer* advance

165   To her, whose worth makes other worthies nothing;
  She is alone.

 Proteus. Then let her alone.

 Valentine. Not for the world. Why, man, she is mine
  own,
  And I as rich in having such a jewel
  As twenty seas, if all their sand were pearl,
170 The water nectar, and the rocks pure gold.
  Forgive me that I do not dream on° thee,
  Because thou see'st me dote upon my love.
  My foolish rival, that her father likes
  Only for his possessions are so huge,
175 Is gone with her along; and I must after,
  For love, thou know'st, is full of jealousy.

 Proteus. But she loves you?

 Valentine. Ay, and we are betrothed; nay, more, our
  marriage hour,
  With all the cunning manner of our flight,
180 Determined of: how I must climb her window,
  The ladder made of cords, and all the means
  Plotted and 'greed on for my happiness.
  Good Proteus, go with me to my chamber,
  In these affairs to aid me with thy counsel.

185 *Proteus.* Go on before; I shall inquire you forth.
  I must unto the road, to disembark
  Some necessaries that I needs must use,
  And then I'll presently attend you.

 Valentine. Will you make haste?

190 *Proteus.* I will.   *Exit* [*Valentine*].
  Even as one heat another heat expels,
  Or as one nail by strength drives out another,
  So the remembrance of my former love
  Is by a newer object quite forgotten.
195 Is it mine eye, or Valentine's praise,
  Her true perfection, or my false transgression,
  That makes me reasonless° to reason thus?

 171 *on* of 197 *reasonless* without justification

She is fair; and so is Julia, that I love—
That I did love, for now my love is thawed,
Which, like a waxen image 'gainst a fire,   200
Bears no impression of the thing it was.
Methinks my zeal to Valentine is cold,
And that I love him not as I was wont.
O, but I love his lady too too much!
And that's the reason I love him so little.   205
How shall I dote on her with more advice,°
That thus without advice begin to love her!
'Tis but her picture° I have yet beheld,
And that hath dazzled my reason's light;
But when I look on her perfections,   210
There is no reason° but I shall be blind.
If I can check my erring love, I will;
If not, to compass° her I'll use my skill.   *Exit.*

Scene V. [*Milan. A street.*]

Enter Speed and Launce [*meeting*].

Speed. Launce! By mine honesty, welcome to Padua!°

Launce. Forswear° not thyself, sweet youth; for I am
not welcome. I reckon this always—that a man is
never undone till he be hanged, nor never welcome
to a place till some certain shot° be paid, and the   5
hostess say "Welcome!"

Speed. Come on, you madcap, I'll to the alehouse with
you presently, where, for one shot of five pence,
thou shalt have five thousand welcomes. But, sirrah,
how did thy master part with Madam Julia?   10

206 *advice* careful thought   208 *picture* i.e., her visible being,
outward appearance   211 *reason* question   213 *compass* get, achieve
II.v.1 *Padua* (apparently Shakespeare forgot that his characters are
in Milan)   2 *Forswear* perjure   5 *shot* alehouse bill

Launce. Marry, after they closed in earnest,° they
parted very fairly in jest.

Speed. But shall she marry him?

Launce. No.

15 *Speed.* How, then? Shall he marry her?

Launce. No, neither.

Speed. What, are they broken?

Launce. No, they are both as whole as a fish.

Speed. Why, then, how stands the matter with them?

20 *Launce.* Marry, thus: when it stands well with him,
it stands well with her.

Speed. What an ass art thou! I understand thee not.

Launce. What a block art thou, that thou canst not!
My staff understands me.

25 *Speed.* What thou sayest?

Launce. Ay, and what I do too. Look thee, I'll but
lean, and my staff understands me.

Speed. It stands under thee, indeed.

Launce. Why, stand-under and under-stand is all one.

30 *Speed.* But tell me true, will't be a match?

Launce. Ask my dog. If he say ay, it will; if he say,
no, it will; if he shake his tail and say nothing, it
will.

Speed. The conclusion is, then, that it will.

35 *Launce.* Thou shalt never get such a secret from me
but by a parable.°

Speed. 'Tis well that I get it so. But, Launce, how say-

---

11 *closed in earnest* (1) formally agreed (2) embraced 36 *by a
parable* i.e., by indirect affirmation

est thou,° that my master is become a notable
lover?

Launce. I never knew him otherwise.   40

Speed. Than how?

Launce. A notable lubber, as thou reportest him to be.

Speed. Why, thou whoreson ass, thou mistak'st me.

Launce. Why fool, I meant not thee; I meant thy
master.   45

Speed. I tell thee, my master is become a hot lover.

Launce. Why, I tell thee, i care not though he burn
himself in love. If thou wilt, go with me to the alehouse; if not, thou art an Hebrew, a Jew, and not
worth the name of a Christian.   50

Speed. Why?

Launce. Because thou hast not so much charity in
thee as to go to the ale with a Christian.° Wilt thou
go?

Speed. At thy service.   *Exeunt.*   55

Scene VI. [*Milan. The Duke's palace.*]

Enter Proteus solus.°

Proteus. To leave my Julia shall I be forsworn;
To love fair Silvia shall I be forsworn;
To wrong my friend, I shall be much forsworn;
And ev'n that pow'r which gave me first my oath
Provokes me to this threefold perjury: 5

37–38 *how sayest thou* what do you think about this   53 *go to the
ale with a Christian* i.e., attend a church-benefit festivity   II.vi.s.d.
solus alone (Latin)

Love bade me swear, and Love bids me forswear.
O sweet-suggesting Love, if thou hast sinned,
Teach me, thy tempted subject, to excuse it!
At first I did adore a twinkling star,
But now I worship a celestial sun.
Unheedful vows may heedfully be broken;
And he wants° wit that wants resolvèd will
To learn° his wit t' exchange the bad for better.
Fie, fie, unreverend tongue! To call her bad,
Whose sovereignty so oft thou hast preferred
With twenty thousand soul-confirming oaths.
I cannot leave to love, and yet I do;
But there I leave to love where I should love.
Julia I lose, and Valentine I lose.
If I keep them, I needs must lose myself;
If I lose them, thus find I by their loss
For Valentine, myself, for Julia, Silvia.
I to myself am dearer than a friend,
For love is still most precious in itself;
And Silvia—witness Heaven, that made her fair!—
Shows Julia but a swarthy Ethiope.
I will forget that Julia is alive,
Rememb'ring that my love to her is dead;
And Valentine I'll hold an enemy,
Aiming at Silvia as a sweeter friend.
I cannot now prove constant to myself,
Without some treachery used to Valentine.
This night he meaneth with a corded ladder
To climb celestial Silvia's chamber window,
Myself in counsel, his competitor.°
Now presently I'll give her father notice
Of their disguising and pretended° flight;
Who, all enraged, will banish Valentine;
For Thurio, he intends, shall wed his daughter.
But, Valentine being gone, I'll quickly cross
By some sly trick blunt Thurio's dull proceeding.
Love, lend me wings to make my purpose swift,
As thou hast lent me wit to plot this drift!°   *Exit.*

12 *wants* lacks 13 *learn* teach 35 *competitor* accomplice 37 *pretended* intended 43 *drift* device

Scene VII. [*Verona. Julia's house.*]

Enter Julia and Lucetta.

Julia. Counsel, Lucetta; gentle girl, assist me;
And, ev'n in kind love, I do conjure thee,
Who art the table° wherein all my thoughts
Are visibly charactered and engraved,
To lesson me, and tell me some good mean,   5
How, with my honor,° I may undertake
A journey to my loving Proteus.

Lucetta. Alas, the way is wearisome and long!

Julia. A true-devoted pilgrim is not weary
To measure kingdoms with his feeble steps;   10
Much less shall she that hath Love's wings to fly—
And when the flight is made to one so dear,
Of such divine perfection, as Sir Proteus.

Lucetta. Better forbear till Proteus make return.

Julia. O, know'st thou not his looks are my soul's
food?   15
Pity the dearth that I have pinèd in
By longing for that food so long a time.
Didst thou but know the inly° touch of love,
Thou wouldst as soon go kindle fire with snow
As seek to quench the fire of love with words.   20

Lucetta. I do not seek to quench your love's hot fire,
But qualify° the fire's extreme rage,
Lest it should burn above the bounds of reason.

Julia. The more thou damm'st it up, the more it burns.
The current that with gentle murmur glides,   25
Thou know'st, being stopped, impatiently doth rage;
But when his fair course is not hinderèd,
He makes sweet music with th' enameled° stones,

II.vii.3 *table* tablet   6 *with my honor* preserving my honor   18 *inly*
inward   22 *qualify* mitigate   28 *enameled* shiny

Giving a gentle kiss to every sedge
30   He overtaketh in his pilgrimage;
And so by many winding nooks he strays,
With willing sport, to the wild ocean.
Then let me go, and hinder not my course.
I'll be as patient as a gentle stream,
35   And make a pastime of each weary step,
Till the last step have brought me to my love;
And there I'll rest, as after much turmoil
A blessèd soul doth in Elysium.

Lucetta. But in what habit° will you go along?

40   *Julia.* Not like a woman, for I would prevent
The loose encounters of lascivious men.
Gentle Lucetta, fit me with such weeds°
As may beseem some well-reputed page.

Lucetta. Why, then, your ladyship must cut your hair.

45   *Julia.* No, girl; I'll knit it up in silken strings
With twenty odd-conceited° truelove knots.
To be fantastic may become a youth
Of greater time° than I shall show to be.

Lucetta. What fashion, madam, shall I make your
breeches?

50   *Julia.* That fits as well as, "Tell me, good my lord,
What compass° will you wear your farthingale?"°
Why, ev'n what fashion thou best likes, Lucetta.

Lucetta. You must needs have them with a codpiece,°
madam.

Julia. Out, out,° Lucetta! That will be ill-favored.

55   *Lucetta.* A round hose, madam, now's not worth a pin,
Unless you have a codpiece to stick pins on.

Julia. Lucetta, as thou lov'st me, let me have

39 *habit* costume   42 *weeds* garments   46 *odd-conceited* ingeniously devised   48 *Of greater time* i.e., older   51 *compass* circum-
ference   51 *farthingale* hooped petticoat   53 *codpiece* pocket or
bag at front of men's breeches (*round hose,* line 55), often fashion-
ably exaggerated   54 *Out, out* fie, fie

What thou think'st meet, and is most mannerly.
But tell me, wench, how will the world repute me
For undertaking so unstaid° a journey?   60
I fear me, it will make me scandalized.

Lucetta. If you think so, then stay at home, and go not.

Julia. Nay, that I will not.

Lucetta. Then never dream on infamy, but go.
If Proteus like your journey when you come,   65
No matter who's displeased when you are gone:
I fear me, he will scarce be pleased withal.°

Julia. That is the least, Lucetta, of my fear.
A thousand oaths, an ocean of his tears,
And instances of infinite° of love   70
Warrant me welcome to my Proteus.

Lucetta. All these are servants to deceitful men.

Julia. Base men, that use them to so base effect!
But truer stars did govern Proteus' birth.
His words are bonds, his oaths are oracles;   75
His love sincere, his thoughts immaculate;
His tears pure messengers sent from his heart;
His heart as far from fraud as heaven from earth.

Lucetta. Pray heav'n he prove so, when you come to
him!

Julia. Now, as thou lov'st me, do him not that wrong,   80
To bear a hard opinion of his truth.
Only deserve my love by loving him,
And presently go with me to my chamber
To take a note of what I stand in need of
To furnish me upon my longing° journey.   85
All that is mine I leave at thy dispose,
My goods, my lands, my reputation;
Only, in lieu thereof, dispatch me hence.
Come, answer not, but to it presently!
I am impatient of my tarriance.   *Exeunt.*   90

60 *unstaid* unbecoming   67 *withal* with   it   70 *infinite* infinity
85 *longing* i.e., occasioned by my longing

ACT III

Scene I. [*Milan. The Duke's palace.*]

Enter Duke, Thurio, [and] Proteus.

Duke. Sir Thurio, give us leave, I pray, awhile;
  We have some secrets to confer about.
                                      [*Exit Thurio.*]
  Now, tell me, Proteus, what's your will with me?

Proteus. My gracious lord, that which I would dis-
      cover°
5   The law of friendship bids me to conceal;
     But when I call to mind your gracious favors
     Done to me, undeserving as I am,
     My duty pricks me on to utter that
     Which else no worldly good should draw from me.
10   Know, worthy prince, Sir Valentine, my friend,
     This night intends to steal away your daughter.
     Myself am one made privy to the plot.
     I know you have determined to bestow her
     On Thurio, whom your gentle daughter hates,
15   And should she thus be stol'n away from you,
     It would be much vexation to your age.
     Thus, for my duty's sake, I rather chose

III.i.4 *discover* disclose

82

To cross my friend in his intended drift
Than, by concealing it, heap on your head
A pack of sorrows which would press you down,   20
Being unprevented, to your timeless° grave.

Duke. Proteus, I thank thee for thine honest care,
Which to requite, command me while I live.
This love of theirs myself have often seen,
Haply when they have judged me fast asleep;   25
And oftentimes have purposed to forbid
Sir Valentine her company and my court.
But, fearing lest my jealous° aim might err,
And so, unworthily disgrace the man,
A rashness that I ever yet have shunned,   30
I gave him gentle looks; thereby to find
That which thyself hast now disclosed to me.
And, that thou mayst perceive my fear of this,
Knowing that tender youth is soon suggested,°
I nightly lodge her in an upper tow'r,   35
The key whereof myself have ever kept;
And thence she cannot be conveyed away.

Proteus. Know, noble lord, they have devised a mean
How he her chamber window will ascend,
And with a corded ladder fetch her down;   40
For which the youthful lover now is gone,
And this way comes he with it presently,
Where, if it please you, you may intercept him.
But, good my lord, do it so cunningly
That my discovery be not aimèd at;°   45
For love of you, not hate unto my friend,
Hath made me publisher of this pretense.°

Duke. Upon mine honor, he shall never know
That I had any light from thee of this.

Proteus. Adieu, my lord; Sir Valentine is coming.   50
                                        [*Exit.*]

---

21 *timeless* untimely   28 *jealous* suspicious   34 *suggested* tempted,
prompted   45 *aimèd at* guessed   47 *pretense* intention

[*Enter Valentine.*]

Duke. Sir Valentine, whither away so fast?

Valentine. Please it your Grace, there is a messenger
  That stays to bear my letters to my friends,
  And I am going to deliver them.

55 *Duke.* Be they of much import?

Valentine. The tenor of them doth but signify
  My health and happy being at your court.

Duke. Nay then, no matter; stay with me awhile.
  I am to break with thee of some affairs
60   That touch me near, wherein thou must be secret.
  'Tis not unknown to thee that I have sought
  To match my friend Sir Thurio to my daughter.

Valentine. I know it well, my lord; and, sure, the
    match
  Were rich and honorable; besides, the gentleman
65   Is full of virtue, bounty, worth, and qualities
  Beseeming such a wife as your fair daughter.
  Cannot your Grace win her to fancy him?

Duke. No, trust me; she is peevish, sullen, froward,°
  Proud, disobedient, stubborn, lacking duty,
70   Neither regarding that she is my child
  Nor fearing me as if I were her father.
  And, may I say to thee, this pride of hers,
  Upon advice,° hath drawn° my love from her;
  And, where I thought the remnant of mine age
75   Should have been cherished by her childlike duty,
  I now am full resolved to take a wife,
  And turn her out to who will take her in.
  Then let her beauty be her wedding dow'r,
  For me and my possessions she esteems not.

Valentine. What would your Grace have me to do in
80   this?

68 *peevish . . . froward* obstinate . . . willful   73 *advice* consideration   73 *drawn* withdrawn

Duke. There is a lady in Verona here°
   Whom I affect; but she is nice° and coy,
   And nought esteems my agèd eloquence.
   Now, therefore, would I have thee to my tutor—
   For long agone I have forgot to court;   *85*
   Besides, the fashion of the time is changed—
   How and which way I may bestow° myself,
   To be regarded in her sun-bright eye.

Valentine. Win her with gifts, if she respect not words.
   Dumb jewels often in their silent kind°   *90*
   More than quick words do move a woman's mind.

Duke. But she did scorn a present that I sent her.

Valentine. A woman sometime scorns what best con-
     tents her.
   Send her another; never give her o'er;
   For scorn at first makes after-love the more.   *95*
   If she do frown, 'tis not in hate of you,
   But rather to beget more love in you.
   If she do chide, 'tis not to have you gone;
   For why, the fools are mad, if left alone.
   Take no repulse, whatever she doth say;   *100*
   For "get you gone," she doth not mean "away!"
   Flatter and praise, commend, extol their graces;
   Though ne'er so black, say they have angels' faces.
   That man that hath a tongue, I say, is no man,
   If with his tongue he cannot win a woman.   *105*

Duke. But she I mean is promised by her friends
   Unto a youthful gentleman of worth,
   And kept severely from resort of men,
   That no man hath access by day to her.

Valentine. Why, then, I would resort to her by night.   *110*

Duke. Ay, but the doors be locked, and keys kept safe,
   That no man hath recourse to her by night.

---

81 *in Verona here* (some editors emend *in* to "of," but probably
Shakespeare forgot his characters are now in Milan)   82 *nice* fastidious   87 *bestow* conduct   90 *kind* nature

Valentine. What lets° but one may enter at her window?

Duke. Her chamber is aloft, far from the ground,
115   And built so shelving° that one cannot climb it
Without apparent hazard of his life.

Valentine. Why, then, a ladder, quaintly made of cords,
To cast up, with a pair of anchoring hooks,
Would serve to scale another Hero's tow'r,
120   So bold Leander would adventure it.

Duke. Now, as thou art a gentleman of blood,°
Advise me where I may have such a ladder.

Valentine. When would you use it? Pray, sir, tell me that.

Duke. This very night; for Love is like a child,
125   That longs for everything that he can come by.

Valentine. By seven o'clock I'll get you such a ladder.

Duke. But, hark thee; I will go to her alone.
How shall I best convey the ladder thither?

Valentine. It will be light, my lord, that you may bear it
130   Under a cloak that is of any length.

Duke. A cloak as long as thine will serve the turn?

Valentine. Ay, my good lord.

Duke.   Then let me see thy cloak.
I'll get me one of such another length.

Valentine. Why, any cloak will serve the turn, my lord.

135 *Duke.* How shall I fashion me to wear a cloak?
I pray thee, let me feel thy cloak upon me.
                              [*Opens Valentine's cloak.*]
What letter is this same? What's here? "To Silvia"—

113 *lets* prevents   115 *shelving* steeply sloping   121 *of blood* i.e.,
of noble blood

And here an engine° fit for my proceeding.
I'll be so bold to break the seal for once.   [*Reads.*]
"My thoughts do harbor with my Silvia nightly;   *140*
   And slaves they are to me, that send them flying.
O, could their master come and go as lightly,
   Himself would lodge where senseless they are
      lying!
My herald thoughts in thy pure bosom rest them,
   While I, their king, that thither them importune,   *145*
Do curse the grace that with such grace hath blessed
      them,
   Because myself do want my servants' fortune.
I curse myself, for they are sent by me,
That they should harbor where their lord should be."
What's here?   *150*
"Silvia, this night I will enfranchise thee."
'Tis so; and here's the ladder for the purpose.
Why, Phaethon—for thou art Merops' son—
Wilt thou aspire to guide the heavenly car,
And with thy daring folly burn the world?°   *155*
Wilt thou reach stars, because they shine on thee?
Go, base intruder! Overweening slave!
Bestow thy fawning smiles on equal mates,
And think my patience, more than thy desert,
Is privilege for thy departure hence.   *160*
Thank me for this more than for all the favors
Which all too much I have bestowed on thee.
But if thou linger in my territories
Longer than swiftest expedition°
Will give thee time to leave our royal court,   *165*
By heaven, my wrath shall far exceed the love
I ever bore my daughter or thyself.
Be gone! I will not hear thy vain excuse;
But, as thou lov'st thy life, make speed from hence.
                                        [*Exit.*]

---

138 *engine* contrivance (here, the ladder)   153–55 *Phaethon . . . the world* (Phaethon's father, Phoebus—not Merops, who was his mother's husband—let the youth drive the horses of the sun across the sky, with dire results)   164 *expedition* speed

Valentine. And why not death rather than living tor-
170   ment?
To die is to be banished from myself;
And Silvia is myself. Banished from her
Is self from self: a deadly banishment!
What light is light, if Silvia be not seen?
175 What joy is joy, if Silvia be not by?—
Unless it be to think that she is by,
And feed upon the shadow° of perfection.
Except I be by Silvia in the night,
There is no music in the nightingale;
180 Unless I look on Silvia in the day,
There is no day for me to look upon.
She is my essence, and I leave° to be,
If I be not by her fair influence°
Fostered, illumined, cherished, kept alive.
185 I fly not death, to fly his deadly doom:
Tarry I here, I but attend on death;
But, fly I hence, I fly away from life.

[*Enter Proteus and Launce.*]

Proteus. Run, boy, run, run, and seek him out.

Launce. Soho, soho!

190 *Proteus.* What seest thou?

Launce. Him we go to find. There's not a hair° on's
head but 'tis a Valentine.°

Proteus. Valentine?

Valentine. No.

195 *Proteus.* Who then? His spirit?

Valentine. Neither.

Proteus. What then?

---

177 *shadow* mere image   182 *leave* cease   183 *influence* i.e., like
that of the stars (see especially Sonnet 15)   191 *hair* (with pun
on "hare," prepared by preceding *Soho,* a hunting cry)   192 *Valentine* (with pun, as in lines 210–14 below)

Valentine. Nothing.

Launce. Can nothing speak? Master, shall I strike?

Proteus. Who wouldst thou strike? *200*

Launce. Nothing.

Proteus. Villain, forbear.

Launce. Why, sir, I'll strike nothing. I pray you—

Proteus. Sirrah, I say, forbear. Friend Valentine, a
word.

Valentine. My ears are stopped, and cannot hear good
news, *205*
So much of bad already hath possessed them.

Proteus. Then in dumb silence will I bury mine,
For they are harsh, untunable, and bad.

Valentine. Is Silvia dead?

Proteus. No, Valentine. *210*

Valentine. No Valentine, indeed, for sacred Silvia.
Hath she forsworn me?

Proteus. No, Valentine.

Valentine. No Valentine, if Silvia have forsworn me.
What is your news? *215*

Launce. Sir, there is a proclamation that you are vanished.

Proteus. That thou art banishèd—O, that's the
news!—
From hence, from Silvia, and from me thy friend.

Valentine. O, I have fed upon this woe already, *220*
And now excess of it will make me surfeit.
Doth Silvia know that I am banishèd?

Proteus. Ay, ay, and she hath offered to the doom—
Which, unreversed, stands in effectual force—
A sea of melting pearl, which some call tears: *225*
Those at her father's churlish feet she tendered

With them, upon her knees, her humble self;
Wringing her hands, whose whiteness so became them
As if but now they waxèd pale for woe.
230   But neither bended knees, pure hands held up,
Sad sighs, deep groans, nor silver-shedding tears,
Could penetrate her uncompassionate sire;
But Valentine, if he be ta'en, must die.
Besides, her intercession chafed him so,
235   When she for thy repeal was suppliant,
That to close prison he commanded her,
With many bitter threats of biding° there.

Valentine. No more; unless the next word that thou speak'st
Have some malignant power upon my life.
240   If so, I pray thee, breathe it in mine ear,
As ending anthem° of my endless dolor.

Proteus. Cease to lament for that thou canst not help,
And study help for that which thou lament'st.
Time is the nurse and breeder of all good.
245   Here if thou stay, thou canst not see thy love;
Besides, thy staying will abridge thy life.
Hope is a lover's staff; walk hence with that,
And manage it against despairing thoughts.
Thy letters may be here, though thou art hence;
250   Which, being writ to me, shall be delivered
Even in the milk-white bosom of thy love.
The time now serves not to expostulate.
Come, I'll convey thee through the city gate,
And, ere I part with thee, confer at large
255   Of all that may concern thy love affairs.
As thou lov'st Silvia, though not for thyself,
Regard thy danger, and along with me!

Valentine. I pray thee, Launce, and if° thou seest my boy,
Bid him make haste, and meet me at the Northgate.

237 *biding* i.e., permanent incarceration   241 *ending anthem* funeral hymn   258 *and if* if

Proteus. Go, sirrah, find him out. Come, Valentine.   260

Valentine. O my dear Silvia! Hapless Valentine!
> [*Exeunt Valentine and Proteus.*]

Launce. I am but a fool, look you, and yet I have the
wit to think my master is a kind of a knave. But
that's all one, if he be but one knave. He lives not
now that knows me to be in love, yet I am in love;   265
but a team of horse shall not pluck that from me,
nor who 'tis I love, and yet 'tis a woman; but what
woman, I will not tell myself, and yet 'tis a milk-
maid; yet 'tis not a maid, for she hath had gossips;°
yet 'tis a maid, for she is her master's maid, and   270
serves for wages. She hath more qualities than a
water spaniel—which is much in a bare Christian.
[*Pulling out a paper*] Here is the cate-log of her
condition. "Imprimis:° She can fetch and carry."
Why, a horse can do no more: nay, a horse cannot   275
fetch, but only carry; therefore is she better than a
jade.° "Item: She can milk"; look you, a sweet virtue in a maid with clean hands.

> [*Enter Speed.*]

Speed. How now, Signior Launce! What news with
your mastership?   280

Launce. With my master's ship? Why, it is at sea.

Speed. Well, your old vice still; mistake the word.
What news, then, in your paper?

Launce. The black'st news that ever thou heard'st.

Speed. Why, man, how black?   285

Launce. Why, as black as ink.

Speed. Let me read them.

Launce. Fie on thee, jolthead!° Thou canst not read.

---

269 *gossips* godparents (for her own child)   274 *Imprimis* in the
first place   277 *jade* nag   288 *jolthead* blockhead

Speed. Thou liest; I can.

290 *Launce.* I will try thee. Tell me this: who begot thee?

Speed. Marry, the son of my grandfather.

Launce. O illiterate loiterer! It was the son of thy grandmother. This proves that thou canst not read.

Speed. Come, fool, come; try me in thy paper.

295 *Launce.* There; and Saint Nicholas° be thy speed!°

Speed. [*Reads*] "Imprimis: She can milk."

Launce. Ay, that she can.

Speed. "Item: She brews good ale."

Launce. And thereof comes the proverb: "Blessing of
300 your heart, you brew good ale."

Speed. "Item: She can sew."

Launce. That's as much as to say, Can she so?

Speed. "Item: She can knit."

Launce. What need a man care for a stock° with a
305 wench when she can knit him a stock?

Speed. "Item: She can wash and scour."

Launce. A special virtue; for then she need not be washed and scoured.

Speed. "Item: She can spin."

310 *Launce.* Then may I set the world on wheels,° when she can spin for her living.

Speed. "Item: She hath many nameless virtues."

Launce. That's as much as to say, bastard virtues—that, indeed, know not their fathers, and therefore
315 have no names.

---

295 *Saint Nicholas* patron saint of scholars (among others)   295
speed aid   304 *stock* dowry (pun follows)   310 *set the world on
wheels* take life easy

Speed. "Here follow her vices."

Launce. Close at the heels of her virtues.

Speed. "Item: She is not to be kissed fasting, in respect of her breath."

Launce. Well, that fault may be mended with a break-   *320*
fast. Read on.

Speed. "Item: She hath a sweet mouth."°

Launce. That makes amends for her sour breath.

Speed. "Item: She doth talk in her sleep."

Launce. It's no matter for that, so she sleep not in her   *325*
talk.

Speed. "Item: She is slow in words."

Launce. O villain, that set this down among her vices!
To be slow in words is a woman's only virtue. I
pray thee, out with't, and place it for her chief   *330*
virtue.

Speed. "Item: She is proud."

Launce. Out with that too; it was Eve's legacy, and
cannot be ta'en from her.

Speed. "Item: She hath no teeth."   *335*

Launce. I care not for that neither, because I love
crusts.

Speed. "Item: She is curst."°

Launce. Well, the best is, she hath no teeth to bite.

Speed. "Item: She will often praise her liquor."   *340*

Launce. If her liquor be good, she shall; if she will
not, I will, for good things should be praised.

Speed. "Item: She is too liberal."

Launce. Of her tongue she cannot, for that's writ down

322 *hath a sweet mouth* i.e., likes sweets   338 *curst* shrewish

345 she is slow of; of her purse she shall not, for that
I'll keep shut. Now, of another thing she may, and
that cannot I help. Well, proceed.

Speed. "Item: She hath more hair than wit, and more
faults than hairs, and more wealth than faults."

350 *Launce.* Stop there; I'll have her. She was mine, and
not mine, twice or thrice in that last article. Rehearse that once more.

Speed. "Item: She hath more hair than wit"—

Launce. More hair than wit? It may be; I'll prove it.
355 The cover of the salt° hides the salt, and therefore
it is more than the salt; the hair that covers the wit
is more than the wit, for the greater hides the less.
What's next?

Speed. "And more faults than hairs"—

360 *Launce.* That's monstrous. O, that that were out!

Speed. "And more wealth than faults."

Launce. Why, that word makes the faults gracious.
Well, I'll have her; and if it be a match, as nothing
is impossible—

365 *Speed.* What then?

Launce. Why, then will I tell thee—that thy master
stays for thee at the Northgate?

Speed. For me?

Launce. For thee! Ay, who art thou? He hath stayed
370 for a better man than thee.

Speed. And must I go to him?

Launce. Thou must run to him, for thou hast stayed
so long that going° will scarce serve the turn.

Speed. Why didst not tell me sooner? Pox of° your
375 love letters!   [*Exit.*]

355 *salt* saltcellar 373 *going* i.e., merely walking 374 *Pox of*
plague (literally, syphilis) on

Launce. Now will he be swinged for reading my letter
—an unmannerly slave, that will thrust himself into
secrets! I'll after, to rejoice in the boy's correction.
                                                    [*Exit.*]

Scene II. [*Milan. The Duke's palace.*]

Enter Duke [*and*] *Thurio.*

Duke. Sir Thurio, fear not but that she will love you,
   Now Valentine is banished from her sight.

Thurio. Since his exile she hath despised me most,
   Forsworn my company, and railed at me,
   That I am desperate of obtaining her.   5

Duke. This weak impress° of love is as a figure
   Trenchèd in ice, which with an hour's heat
   Dissolves to water, and doth lose his form.
   A little time will melt her frozen thoughts,
   And worthless Valentine shall be forgot.   10

[*Enter Proteus.*]

   How now, Sir Proteus! Is your countryman,
   According to our proclamation, gone?

Proteus. Gone, my good lord.

Duke. My daughter takes his going grievously.

Proteus. A little time, my lord, will kill that grief.   15

Duke. So I believe, but Thurio thinks not so.
   Proteus, the good conceit° I hold of thee—
   For thou hast shown some sign of good desert—
   Makes me the better to confer with thee.

III.ii.6 *impress* impression (dent, groove)   17 *conceit* opinion

20   *Proteus.* Longer than I prove loyal to your Grace,
     Let me not live to look upon your Grace.

Duke. Thou know'st how willingly I would effect
     The match between Sir Thurio and my daughter.

Proteus. I do, my lord.

25   *Duke.* And also, I think, thou art not ignorant
     How she opposes her against my will.

Proteus. She did, my lord, when Valentine was here.

Duke. Ay, and perversely she persevers so.
     What might we do to make the girl forget
30   The love of Valentine, and love Sir Thurio?

Proteus. The best way is to slander Valentine
     With falsehood, cowardice, and poor descent,
     Three things that women highly hold in hate.

Duke. Ay, but she'll think that it is spoke in hate.

35   *Proteus.* Ay, if his enemy deliver it;
     Therefore it must with circumstance° be spoken
     By one whom she esteemeth as his friend.

Duke. Then you must undertake to slander him.

Proteus. And that, my lord, I shall be loath to do.
40   'Tis an ill office for a gentleman,
     Especially against his very friend.

Duke. Where your good word cannot advantage him,
     Your slander never can endamage him;
     Therefore the office is indifferent,°
45   Being entreated to it by your friend.

Proteus. You have prevailed, my lord. If I can do it
     By aught that I can speak in his dispraise,
     She shall not long continue love to him.
     But say this weed her love from Valentine,
50   It follows not that she will love Sir Thurio.

Thurio. Therefore, as you unwind her love from him,

36 *circumstance* circumstantial detail   44 *indifferent* neutral in
effect

Lest it should ravel and be good to none,
You must provide to bottom° it on me;
Which must be done by praising me as much
As you in worth dispraise Sir Valentine.   55

Duke. And, Proteus, we dare trust you in this kind,°
Because we know, on Valentine's report,
You are already Love's firm votary
And cannot soon revolt and change your mind.
Upon this warrant shall you have access   60
Where you with Silvia may confer at large;
For she is lumpish, heavy, melancholy,
And, for your friend's sake, will be glad of you;
Where you may temper° her by your persuasion
To hate young Valentine and love my friend.   65

Proteus. As much as I can do, I will effect.
But you, Sir Thurio, are not sharp enough;
You must lay lime to tangle° her desires
By wailful sonnets, whose composèd rhymes
Should be full-fraught with serviceable vows.°   70

Duke. Ay,
Much is the force of heaven-bred poesy.

Proteus. Say that upon the altar of her beauty
You sacrifice your tears, your sighs, your heart.
Write till your ink be dry, and with your tears   75
Moist it again, and frame some feeling line
That may discover such integrity.°
For Orpheus' lute was strung with poets' sinews,
Whose golden touch could soften steel and stones,
Make tigers tame, and huge leviathans   80
Forsake unsounded deeps to dance on sands.°
After your dire-lamenting elegies,
Visit by night your lady's chamber window

53 *bottom* anchor, tie (as a weaver's thread)   56 *kind* i.e., an affair of this nature   64 *temper* make pliant, shape   68 *lime to tangle* birdlime to ensnare (birdlime is a sticky substance spread on branches to catch birds)   70 *full-fraught with serviceable vows* loaded with vows to serve faithfully   77 *discover such integrity* exhibit such devotion   78–81 *Orpheus' lute . . . sands* (cf. *Merchant of Venice*, V.i for a simpler tribute to the musician of Thrace)

With some sweet consort;° to their instruments
85 Tune a deploring dump.° The night's dead silence
Will well become such sweet-complaining griev-
    ance.
This, or else nothing, will inherit° her.

Duke. This discipline° shows thou hast been in love.

Thurio. And thy advice this night I'll put in practice.
90 Therefore, sweet Proteus, my direction-giver,
Let us into the city presently
To sort° some gentlemen well skilled in music.
I have a sonnet that will serve the turn
To give the onset° to thy good advice.

95 *Duke.* About it, gentlemen!

Proteus. We'll wait upon your Grace till after supper,
And afterward determine our proceedings.

Duke. Even now about it! I will pardon you.   *Exeunt.*

---

84 *sweet consort* i.e., company of musicians   85 *deploring dump*
doleful ditty   87 *inherit* obtain   88 *discipline* instruction   92 *sort*
sort out, select   94 *give the onset* make a beginning

ACT IV

Scene I. [*A forest.*]

Enter certain Outlaws.

First Outlaw. Fellows, stand fast; I see a passenger.°

Second Outlaw. If there be ten, shrink not, but down
    with 'em.

[*Enter Valentine and Speed.*]

Third Outlaw. Stand, sir, and throw us that° you have
    about ye.
  If not, we'll make you sit, and rifle you.

Speed. Sir, we are undone; these are the villains   *5*
  That all the travelers do fear so much.

Valentine. My friends—

First Outlaw. That's not so, sir; we are your enemies.

Second Outlaw. Peace! We'll hear him.

Third Outlaw. Ay, by my beard, will we, for he's a
    proper° man.   *10*

Valentine. Then know that I have little wealth to lose.

IV.i.1 *passenger* pedestrian   3 *that* that which   10 *proper* handsome

A man I am crossed with adversity.
My riches are these poor habiliments,
Of which if you should here disfurnish° me,
15   You take the sum and substance that I have.

Second Outlaw. Whitner travel you?

Valentine. To Verona.

First Outlaw. Whence came you?

Valentine. From Milan.

20   *Third Outlaw.* Have you long sojourned there?

Valentine. Some sixteen months, and longer might
    have stayed
    If crooked fortune had not thwarted me.

First Outlaw. What, were you banished thence?

Valentine. I was.

25   *Second Outlaw.* For what offense?

Valentine. For that which now torments me to re-
    hearse:
    I killed a man, whose death I much repent;
    But yet I slew him manfully in fight,
    Without false vantage° or base treachery.

30   *First Outlaw.* Why, ne'er repent it, if it were done so.
    But were you banished for so small a fault?

Valentine. I was, and held me glad of such a doom.°

Second Outlaw. Have you the tongues?°

Valentine. My youthful travel therein made me
    happy,°
35   Or else I often had been miserable.

Third Outlaw. By the bare scalp of Robin Hood's fat
    friar,
    This fellow were a king for our wild faction!

14 *disfurnish* deprive   29 *false vantage* i.e., such advantage as is
gained by deceit   32 *doom* sentence   33 *Have you the tongues*
do you know foreign languages   34 *happy* fortunate

First Outlaw. We'll have him. Sirs, a word.

Speed. Master, be one of them; it's an honorable kind
   of thievery.   40

Valentine. Peace, villain!

Second Outlaw. Tell us this: have you anything to
   take to?°

Valentine. Nothing but my fortune.

Third Outlaw. Know, then, that some of us are gen-
   tlemen,
   Such as the fury of ungoverned youth   45
   Thrust from the company of awful° men:
   Myself was from Verona banishèd
   For practicing° to steal away a lady,
   An heir, and near allied unto the Duke.

Second Outlaw. And I from Mantua, for a gentleman   50
   Who, in my mood, I stabbed unto the heart.

First Outlaw. And I for suchlike petty crimes as these.
   But to the purpose—for we cite our faults,
   That they may hold excused our lawless lives;
   And partly, seeing you are beautified   55
   With goodly shape, and by your own report
   A linguist, and a man of such perfection
   As we do in our quality much want°—

Second Outlaw. Indeed, because you are a banished
   man,
   Therefore, above the rest, we parley to you.   60
   Are you content to be our general,
   To make a virtue of necessity,
   And live, as we do, in this wilderness?

Third Outlaw. What say'st thou? Wilt thou be of our
   consort?
   Say ay, and be the captain of us all.   65

_____

42 *anything to take to* any trade to take up   46 *awful* deeply
respectful (but possibly a printer's slip for "lawful")   48 *prac-
ticing* plotting   58 *in our quality much want* much lack in our profession

We'll do thee homage and be ruled by thee,
Love thee as our commander and our king.

First Outlaw. But if thou scorn our courtesy, thou
diest.

Second Outlaw. Thou shalt not live to brag what we
have offered.

70 *Valentine.* I take your offer, and will live with you,
Provided that you do no outrages
On silly° women or poor passengers.

Third Outlaw. No, we detest such vile base practices.
Come, go with us; we'll bring thee to our crews
75 And show thee all the treasure we have got,
Which, with ourselves, all rest at thy dispose.

Exeunt.

Scene II. [*Milan. Beneath Silvia's window.*]

Enter Proteus.

Proteus. Already have I been false to Valentine,
And now I must be as unjust to Thurio.
Under the color° of commending him,
I have access my own love to prefer.°
5 But Silvia is too fair, too true, too holy
To be corrupted with my worthless gifts.
When I protest true loyalty to her,
She twits me with my falsehood to my friend;
When to her beauty I commend my vows,
10 She bids me think how I have been forsworn
In breaking faith with Julia whom I loved.
And notwithstanding all her sudden quips,
The least whereof would quell a lover's hope,
Yet, spaniel-like, the more she spurns my love,

72 *silly* defenseless   IV.ii.3 *color* pretense   4 *prefer* advance

The more it grows, and fawneth on her still.   15
But here comes Thurio; now must we to her window
And give some evening music to her ear.

[*Enter Thurio and Musicians.*]

Thurio. How now, Sir Proteus, are you crept before
    us?

Proteus. Ay, gentle Thurio, for you know that love
    Will creep in service where it cannot go.°   20

Thurio. Ay, but I hope, sir, that you love not here.

Proteus. Sir, but I do; or else I would be hence.

Thurio. Who? Silvia?

Proteus.   Ay, Silvia, for your sake.

Thurio. I thank you for your own. Now, gentlemen,
    Let's tune, and to it lustily awhile.   25

[*Enter, at a distance, Host, and Julia in boy's
    clothes.*]

Host, Now, my young guest, methinks you're ally-
    cholly.° I pray you, why is it?

Julia. Marry, mine host, because I cannot be merry.

Host. Come, we'll have you merry. I'll bring you where
    you shall hear music, and see the gentleman that   30
    you asked for.

Julia. But shall I hear him speak?

Host. Ay, that you shall.

Julia. That will be music.   [*Music plays.*]

Host. Hark, hark!   35

Julia. Is he among these?

Host. Ay, but, peace! Let's hear 'em.

20 *go* walk upright   26–27 *allycholly* i.e., melancholy

Song.

Who is Silvia, what is she,
  That all our swains commend her?
40 Holy, fair, and wise is she;
  The heaven such grace did lend her,
That she might admirèd be.

Is she kind as she is fair?
  For beauty lives with kindness.
45 Love doth to her eyes repair,
  To help him of his blindness,
And, being helped, inhabits there.

Then to Silvia let us sing,
  That Silvia is excelling;
50 She excels each mortal thing
  Upon the dull earth dwelling.
To her let us garlands bring.

Host. How now! Are you sadder than you were before?
How do you, man? The music likes° you not.

55 *Julia.* You mistake; the musician likes me not.

Host. Why, my pretty youth?

Julia. He plays false, father.

Host. How? Out of tune on the strings?

Julia. Not so; but yet so false that he grieves my very
60 heartstrings.

Host. You have a quick ear.

Julia. Ay, I would I were deaf; it makes me have a
slow° heart.

Host. I perceive you delight not in music.

65 *Julia.* Not a whit, when it jars so.

54 *likes* pleases   63 *slow* i.e., heavy

Host. Hark, what fine change° is in the music!

Julia. Ay, that change is the spite.

Host. You would have them always play but one thing?

Julia. I would always have one play but one thing.
But, host, doth this Sir Proteus that we talk on   *70*
Often resort unto this gentlewoman?

Host. I tell you what Launce, his man, told me—he
loved her out of all nick.°

Julia. Where is Launce?

Host. Gone to seek his dog, which tomorrow, by his   *75*
master's command, he must carry for a present to
his lady.

Julia. Peace! Stand aside. The company parts.

Proteus. Sir Thurio, fear not you. I will so plead
That you shall say my cunning drift excels.   *80*

Thurio. Where meet we?

Proteus.   At Saint Gregory's well.

Thurio.   Farewell.
                    [*Exeunt Thurio and Musicians.*]

                    [*Enter Silvia above.*]

Proteus. Madam, good even to your ladyship.

Silvia. I thank you for your music, gentlemen.
Who is that that spake?

Proteus. One, lady, if you knew his pure heart's truth,   *85*
You would quickly learn to know him by his voice.

Silvia. Sir Proteus, as I take it.

Proteus. Sir Proteus, gentle lady, and your servant.

66 *change* modulation (in the next line Julia puns, alluding to
the change in Proteus' affections)   73 *out of all nick* beyond
measure

Silvia. What's your will?

Proteus.   That I may compass yours.

90 *Silvia.* You have your wish; my will is even this:
That presently you hie you home to bed.
Thou subtle, perjured, false, disloyal man!
Think'st thou I am so shallow, so conceitless,°
To be seducèd by thy flattery,
95 That hast deceived so many with thy vows?
Return, return, and make thy love amends.
For me, by this pale queen of night I swear,
I am so far from granting thy request
That I despise thee for thy wrongful suit,
100 And by and by intend to chide myself
Even for this time I spend in talking to thee.

Proteus. I grant, sweet love, that I did love a lady;
But she is dead.

Julia. [*Aside*] 'Twere false, if I should speak it,
105 For I am sure she is not burièd.

Silvia. Say that she be; yet Valentine thy friend
Survives, to whom, thyself art witness,
I am betrothed. And art thou not ashamed
To wrong him with thy importunacy?

110 *Proteus.* I likewise hear that Valentine is dead.

Silvia. And so suppose am I, for in his grave
Assure thyself my love is burièd.

Proteus. Sweet lady, let me rake it from the earth.

Silvia. Go to thy lady's grave, and call hers thence;
115 Or, at the least, in hers sepulcher thine.

Julia. [*Aside*] He heard not that.

Proteus. Madam, if your heart be so obdurate,
Vouchsafe° me yet your picture for my love,
The picture that is hanging in your chamber.
120 To that I'll speak, to that I'll sigh and weep;
For since the substance of your perfect self

93 *conceitless* witless   118 *Vouchsafe* grant

Is else devoted,° I am but a shadow,
And to your shadow° will I make true love.

Julia. [*Aside*] If 'twere a substance, you would, sure,
  deceive it,
And make it but a shadow, as I am.   *125*

Silvia. I am very loath to be your idol, sir;
But since your falsehood shall become you well
To worship shadows and adore false shapes,
Send to me in the morning, and I'll send it.
And so, good rest.

Proteus.   As wretches have o'ernight   *130*
That wait for execution in the morn.
            [*Exeunt Proteus and Silvia severally.*]

Julia. Host, will you go?

Host. By my halidom,° I was fast asleep.

Julia. Pray you, where lies° Sir Proteus?

Host. Marry, at my house. Trust me, I think 'tis almost *135*
  day.

Julia. Not so; but it hath been the longest night
That e'er I watched, and the most heaviest.

                                          [*Exeunt.*]

Scene III. [*Milan. Beneath Silvia's window.*]

Enter Eglamour.

Eglamour. This is the hour that Madam Silvia
Entreated me to call and know her mind.
There's some great matter she'd employ me in.
Madam, madam!

122 *else devoted* vowed to someone else   123 *shadow* portrait
133 *halidom* sacred relic (a mild oath)   134 *lies* lodges

[*Enter Silvia above.*]

Silvia. Who calls?

5 *Eglamour.*   Your servant and your friend,
   One that attends your ladyship's command.

Silvia. Sir Eglamour, a thousand times good morrow.

Eglamour. As many, worthy lady, to yourself.
   According to your ladyship's impose,°
10 I am thus early come to know what service
   It is your pleasure to command me in.

Silvia. O Eglamour, thou art a gentleman—
   Think not I flatter, for I swear I do not—
   Valiant, wise, remorseful,° well accomplished.
15 Thou art not ignorant what dear good will
   I bear unto the banished Valentine,
   Nor how my father would enforce me marry
   Vain Thurio, whom my very soul abhors.
   Thyself hast loved, and I have heard thee say
20 No grief did ever come so near thy heart
   As when thy lady and thy true love died,
   Upon whose grave thou vow'dst pure chastity.
   Sir Eglamour, I would to Valentine,
   To Mantua, where I hear he makes abode;
25 And, for the ways are dangerous to pass,
   I do desire thy worthy company,
   Upon whose faith and honor I repose.
   Urge not my father's anger, Eglamour,
   But think upon my grief, a lady's grief,
30 And on the justice of my flying hence
   To keep me from a most unholy match,
   Which heaven and fortune still rewards with plagues.
   I do desire thee, even from a heart
   As full of sorrows as the sea of sands,
35 To bear me company, and go with me:
   If not, to hide what I have said to thee,
   That I may venture to depart alone.

Eglamour. Madam, I pity much your grievances,

IV.iii.9 *impose* command   14 *remorseful* compassionate

Which since I know they virtuously are placed,
I give consent to go along with you,   *40*
Recking as little what betideth me
As much I wish all good befortune you.
When will you go?

Silvia.   This evening coming.

Eglamour. Where shall I meet you?

Silvia.   At Friar Patrick's cell,
Where I intend holy confession.   *45*

Eglamour. I will not fail your ladyship. Good morrow,
gentle lady.

Silvia. Good morrow, kind Sir Eglamour.
                                Exeunt [severally].

Scene IV. [*Milan. Beneath Silvia's window.*]

Enter Launce, [with his dog].

Launce. When a man's servant shall play the cur with
him, look you, it goes hard: one that I brought up
of° a puppy; one that I saved from drowning, when
three or four of his blind brothers and sisters went
to it! I have taught him, even as one would say pre-   *5*
cisely, "thus I would teach a dog." I was sent to
deliver him as a present to Mistress Silvia from my
master, and I came no sooner into the dining chamber, but he steps me to her trencher° and steals her
capon's leg. O, 'tis a foul thing when a cur cannot   *10*
keep° himself in all companies! I would have, as
one should say, one that takes upon him to be a
dog indeed, to be as it were, a dog at all things. If
I had not had more wit than he, to take a fault upon
me that he did, I think verily he had been hanged   *15*

IV.iv.3 *of* from   9 *trencher* wooden plate   11 *keep* control

for't; sure as I live, he had suffered for't. You shall
judge. He thrusts me himself into the company of
three or four gentlemanlike dogs under the Duke's
table; he had not been there—bless the mark!—a
20 pissing while, but all the chamber smelt him. "Out
with the dog!" says one. "What cur is that?" says
another. "Whip him out," says the third. "Hang him
up," says the Duke. I, having been acquainted with
the smell before, knew it was Crab, and goes me to
25 the fellow that whips the dogs. "Friend," quoth I,
"you mean to whip the dog?" "Ay, marry, do I,"
quoth he. "You do him the more wrong," quoth I;
" 'twas I did the thing you wot° of." He makes me
no more ado, but whips me out of the chamber.
30 How many masters would do this for his servant?
Nay, I'll be sworn, I have sat in the stocks for pud-
dings° he hath stol'n; otherwise he had been exe-
cuted. I have stood on the pillory for geese he hath
killed; otherwise he had suffered for't. Thou think'st
35 not of this now. Nay, I remember the trick you
served me when I took my leave of Madam Silvia.
Did not I bid thee still mark me, and do as I do?
When didst thou see me heave up my leg, and make
water against a gentlewoman's farthingale? Didst
40 thou ever see me do such a trick?

[*Enter Proteus and Julia.*]

Proteus. Sebastian is thy name? I like thee well.
    And will employ thee in some service presently.

Julia. In what you please. I'll do what I can.

Proteus. I hope thou wilt. [*To Launce*] How now, you
    whoreson peasant!
45 Where have you been these two days loitering?

Launce. Marry, sir, I carried Mistress Silvia the dog
    you bade me.

Proteus. And what says she to my little jewel?

28 *wot* know   31–32 *puddings* sausages

Launce. Marry, she says your dog was a cur, and tells
   you currish thanks is good enough for such a present.   *50*

Proteus. But she received my dog?

Launce. No, indeed, did she not. Here have I brought
   him back again.

Proteus. What, didst thou offer her this from me?

Launce. Ay, sir. The other squirrel° was stol'n from   *55*
   me by the hangman's boys° in the market place, and
   then I offered her mine own, who is a dog as big
   as ten of yours, and therefore the gift the greater.

Proteus. Go get thee hence and find my dog again,
   Or ne'er return again into my sight.
   Away, I say! Stayest thou to vex me here?   *60*
                              [*Exit Launce.*]
   A slave, that still an end° turns me to shame!
   Sebastian, I have entertainèd° thee
   Partly that° I have need of such a youth
   That can with some discretion do my business,   *65*
   For 'tis no trusting to yond foolish lout;
   But chiefly for thy face and thy behavior,
   Which, if my augury deceive me not,
   Witness good bringing up, fortune, and truth.
   Therefore, know thou, for this I entertain thee.   *70*
   Go presently, and take this ring with thee;
   Deliver it to Madam Silvia.
   She loved me well delivered it to me.

Julia. It seems you loved not her, to leave her token.
   She is dead, belike?

Proteus.   Not so; I think she lives.   *75*

Julia. Alas!

Proteus. Why dost thou cry "Alas"?

---

55 *squirrel* i.e., little dog 56 *hangman's boys* i.e., boys who
will surely belong to the hangman (hang) at last 62 *still an end*
forevermore 63 *entertainèd* retained 64 *Partly that* in part
because

Julia.   I cannot choose
  But pity her.

Proteus.   Wherefore shouldst thou pity her?

Julia. Because methinks that she loved you as well
80   As you do love your lady Silvia.
   She dreams on him that has forgot her love;
   You dote on her that cares not for your love.
   'Tis pity love should be so contrary;
   And thinking on it makes me cry "Alas!"

85 *Proteus.* Well, give her that ring, and therewithal
   This letter. That's her chamber. Tell my lady
   I claim the promise for her heavenly picture.
   Your message done, hie home unto my chamber,
   Where thou shalt find me, sad and solitary.   [*Exit.*]

90 *Julia.* How many women would do such a message?
   Alas, poor Proteus! Thou hast entertained
   A fox to be the shepherd of thy lambs.
   Alas, poor fool! Why do I pity him
   That with his very heart despiseth me?
95   Because he loves her, he despiseth me;
   Because I love him, I must pity him.
   This ring I gave him when he parted from me,
   To bind him to remember my good will;
   And now am I, unhappy messenger,
100   To plead for that which I would not obtain,
   To carry that which I would have refused,
   To praise his faith which I would have dispraised.
   I am my master's true-confirmèd love,
   But cannot be true servant to my master
105   Unless I prove false traitor to myself.
   Yet will I woo for him, but yet so coldly
   As, heaven it knows, I would not have him speed.°

[*Enter Silvia, attended.*]

  Gentlewoman, good day! I pray you, be my mean
  To bring me where to speak with Madam Silvia.

107 *speed* prosper, succeed

Silvia. What would you with her, if that I be she?   *110*

Julia. If you be she, I do entreat your patience
To hear me speak the message I am sent on.

Silvia. From whom?

Julia. From my master, Sir Proteus, madam.

Silvia. O, he sends you for a picture.   *115*

Julia. Ay, madam.

Silvia. Ursula, bring my picture there.
Go give your master this. Tell him, from me,
One Julia, that his changing thoughts forget,
Would better fit his chamber than this shadow.   *120*

Julia. Madam, please you peruse this letter—
Pardon me, madam; I have unadvised°
Delivered you a paper that I should not.
This is the letter to your ladyship.

Silvia. I pray thee, let me look on that again.   *125*

Julia. It may not be; good madam, pardon me.

Silvia. There, hold!
I will not look upon your master's lines.
I know they are stuffed with protestations,
And full of new-found oaths which he will break   *130*
As easily as I do tear his paper.

Julia. Madam, he sends your ladyship this ring.

Silvia. The more shame for him that he sends it me,
For I have heard him say a thousand times
His Julia gave it him at his departure.   *135*
Though his false finger have profaned the ring,
Mine shall not do his Julia so much wrong.

Julia. She thanks you.

Silvia. What say'st thou?

Julia. I thank you, madam, that you tender her.°   *140*

122 *unadvised* unintentionally   140 *tender her* i.e., have a care for
her interest

Poor gentlewoman! My master wrongs her much.

Silvia. Dost thou know her?

Julia. Almost as well as I do know myself.
To think upon her woes, I do protest
145 That I have wept a hundred several° times.

Silvia. Belike she thinks that Proteus hath forsook her.

Julia. I think she doth; and that's her cause of sorrow.

Silvia. Is she not passing° fair?

Julia. She hath been fairer, madam, than she is.
150 When she did think my master loved her well,
She, in my judgment, was as fair as you.
But since she did neglect her looking glass,
And threw her sun-expelling mask away,
The air hath starved the roses in her cheeks
155 And pinched the lily-tincture of her face,
That now she is become as black° as I.

Silvia. How tall was she?

Julia. About my stature: for, at Pentecost,°
When all our pageants of delight were played,
160 Our youth got me to play the woman's part,
And I was trimmed in Madam Julia's gown,
Which servèd me as fit, by all men's judgments,
As if the garment had been made for me.
Therefore I know she is about my height.
165 And at that time I made her weep agood,°
For I did play a lamentable part.
Madam, 'twas Ariadne° passioning
For Theseus' perjury and unjust flight,
Which I so lively acted with my tears
170 That my poor mistress, movèd therewithal,
Wept bitterly; and would I might be dead

145 *several* separate 148 *passing* surpassingly 156 *black* i.e.,
from the sun 158 *Pentecost* (Whitsunday [seventh Sunday after
Easter], an occasion for morris dances, "pageants of delight," and
such outdoor festivities) 165 *agood* aplenty 167 *Ariadne* (daughter of King Minos, who aided Theseus' flight from the Cretan laby-
rinth, only to be abandoned on the isle of Naxos)

  If I in thought felt not her very sorrow!

Silvia. She is beholding° to thee, gentle youth.
  Alas, poor lady, desolate and left!
  I weep myself to think upon thy words.
  Here, youth, there is my purse. I give thee this   175
  For thy sweet mistress' sake, because thou lov'st her.
  Farewell.   [*Exit Silvia, with attendants.*]

Julia. And she shall thank you for't, if e'er you know
      her.
  A virtuous gentlewoman, mild and beautiful!   180
  I hope my master's suit will be but cold,
  Since she respects my mistress' love so much.
  Alas, how love can trifle with itself!
  Here is her picture: let me see; I think,
  If I had such a tire,° this face of mine   185
  Were full as lovely as is this of hers.
  And yet the painter flattered her a little,
  Unless I flatter with myself too much.
  Her hair is auburn, mine is perfect yellow:
  If that be all the difference in his love,   190
  I'll get me such a colored periwig.
  Her eyes are gray as glass, and so are mine:
  Ay, but her forehead's low, and mine's as high.
  What should it be that he respects in her,
  But I can make respective° in myself,   195
  If this fond Love° were not a blinded god?
  Come, shadow, come, and take this shadow up,°
  For 'tis thy rival. O thou senseless form,
  Thou shalt be worshiped, kissed, loved, and adored!
  And, were there sense in his idolatry,   200
  My substance should be statue in thy stead.
  I'll use thee kindly for thy mistress' sake,
  That used me so; or else, by Jove I vow,
  I should have scratched out your unseeing eyes,
  To make my master out of love with thee!   *Exit.*   205

173 *beholding* indebted   185 *tire* headdress   195 *respective* worthy
of respect   196 *fond Love* i.e., foolish Cupid   197 *Come . . .
shadow up* come, shadow (of my former self), and "take on" this
other shadow (Silvia's portrait)

ACT V

Scene I. [*Milan. An abbey.*]

Enter Eglamour.

Eglamour. The sun begins to gild the western sky,
And now it is about the very hour
That Silvia, at Friar Patrick's cell, should meet me.
She will not fail, for lovers break not hours,
5   Unless it be to come before their time,
So much they spur their expedition.
See where she comes.

[*Enter Silvia.*]

           Lady, a happy evening!

Silvia. Amen, amen! Go on, good Eglamour,
Out at the postern° by the abbey wall.
10   I fear I am attended° by some spies.

Eglamour. Fear not; the forest is not three leagues off.
If we recover° that, we are sure enough.   *Exeunt.*

V.i.9 *postern* small door at side or rear 10 *attended* followed
12 *recover* reach

116

Scene II. [*Milan. The Duke's palace.*]

Enter Thurio, Proteus, [and] Julia.

Thurio. Sir Proteus, what says Silvia to my suit?

Proteus. O, sir, I find her milder than she was;
   And yet she takes exceptions at your person.

Thurio. What, that my leg is too long?

Proteus. No; that it is too little.   5

Thurio. I'll wear a boot, to make it somewhat rounder.

Julia. [*Aside*] But love will not be spurred° to what
   it loathes.

Thurio. What says she to my face?

Proteus. She says it is a fair one.

Thurio. Nay then, the wanton lies; my face is black.   10

Proteus. But pearls are fair; and the old saying is,
   Black men are pearls in beauteous ladies' eyes.

Julia. [*Aside*] 'Tis true, such pearls as put out ladies'
   eyes;
   For I had rather wink than look on them.

Thurio. How likes she my discourse?°   15

Proteus. Ill, when you talk of war.

Thurio. But well, when I discourse of love and peace?

Julia. [*Aside*] But better, indeed, when you hold your
   peace.

V.ii.7 *spurred* (with reference to preceding "boot")   15 *discourse*
conversational ability

Thurio. What says she to my valor?

20 *Proteus.* O, sir, she makes no doubt of that.

Julia. [*Aside*] She needs not, when she knows it cow-
   ardice.

Thurio. What says she to my birth?

Proteus. That you are well derived.

Julia. [*Aside*] True, from a gentleman to a fool.

25 *Thurio.* Considers she my possessions?

Proteus. O, ay, and pities them.

Thurio. Wherefore?

Julia. [*Aside*] That such an ass should owe° them.

Proteus. That they are out by lease.°

30 *Julia.* Here comes the Duke.

[*Enter Duke.*]

Duke. How now, Sir Proteus! How now, Thurio!
   Which of you saw Sir Eglamour of late?

Thurio. Not I.

Proteus.   Nor I.

Duke.   Saw you my daughter?

Proteus.   Neither.

Duke. Why then,
35   She's fled unto that peasant Valentine,
   And Eglamour is in her company.
   'Tis true; for Friar Laurence met them both
   As he in penance wandered through the forest.
   Him he knew well, and guessed that it was she,
40   But, being masked, he was not sure of it;
   Besides, she did intend confession
   At Patrick's cell this even, and there she was not.

28 *owe* own   29 *out by lease* i.e., because Thurio is such a fool,
he will surely hold onto his possessions only temporarily

These likelihoods confirm her flight from hence.
Therefore, I pray you, stand not to discourse,
But mount you presently, and meet with me   45
Upon the rising of the mountain foot°
That leads toward Mantua, whither they are fled.
Dispatch, sweet gentlemen, and follow me.   [*Exit.*]

Thurio. Why, this it is to be a peevish girl
That flies her fortune when it follows her.
I'll after, more to be revenged on Eglamour   50
Than for the love of reckless Silvia.   [*Exit.*]

Proteus. And I will follow, more for Silvia's love
Than hate of Eglamour, that goes with her.   [*Exit.*]

Julia. And I will follow, more to cross that love   55
Than hate for Silvia, that is gone for love.   [*Exit.*]

Scene III. [*A forest.*]

[*Enter*] Silvia [*and*] Outlaws.

First Outlaw. Come, come,
Be patient; we must bring you to our captain.

Silvia. A thousand more mischances than this one
Have learned me how to brook° this patiently.

Second Outlaw. Come, bring her away.   5

First Outlaw. Where is the gentleman that was with
her?

Third Outlaw. Being nimble footed, he hath outrun us,
But Moyses and Valerius follow him.
Go thou with her to the west end of the wood;
There is our captain. We'll follow him that's fled;   10
The thicket is beset;° he cannot 'scape.

46 *rising of the mountain foot* i.e., foothill   V.iii.4 *learned me how
to brook* taught me how to endure   **11** *beset* surrounded

First Outlaw. Come, I must bring you to our captain's
       cave.
 Fear not; he bears an honorable mind,
 And will not use a woman lawlessly.

15 *Silvia.* O Valentine, this I endure for thee!   *Exeunt.*

Scene IV. [*Another part of the forest.*]

Enter Valentine.

Valentine. How use° doth breed a habit in a man!
 This shadowy desert,° unfrequented woods,
 I better brook than flourishing peopled towns.
 Here can I sit alone, unseen of any,
5 And to the nightingale's complaining notes
 Tune my distresses and record my woes.
 O thou that dost inhabit in my breast,
 Leave not the mansion so long tenantless,
 Lest, growing ruinous, the building fall,
10 And leave no memory of what it was!
 Repair me with thy presence, Silvia;
 Thou gentle nymph, cherish thy forlorn swain!
         [*Noise within.*]
 What halloing and what stir is this today?
 These are my mates, that make their wills their law,
15 Have° some unhappy passenger in chase.
 They love me well; yet I have much to do
 To keep them from uncivil outrages.
 Withdraw thee, Valentine. Who's this comes here?
         [*Retires.*]

[*Enter Proteus, Silvia, and Julia.*]

Proteus. Madam, this service I have done for you—
20   Though you respect not aught your servant doth—

V.iv.1 *use* custom   2 *shadowy desert* wild place inhabited only with
shadows (of trees)   15 *Have* who have

   To hazard life, and rescue you from him
   That would have forced your honor and your love.
   Vouchsafe me, for my meed, but one fair look;
   A smaller boon than this I cannot beg,
   And less than this, I am sure, you cannot give.   25

Valentine. [*Aside*] How like a dream is this I see and
      hear!
   Love, lend me patience to forbear awhile.

Silvia. O miserable, unhappy that I am!

Proteus. Unhappy were you, madam, ere I came;
   But by my coming I have made you happy.   30

Silvia. By thy approach thou mak'st me most unhappy.

Julia. [*Aside*] And me, when he approacheth to your
      presence.

Silvia. Had I been seizèd by a hungry lion,
   I would have been a breakfast to the beast
   Rather than have false Proteus rescue me.   35
   O, Heaven be judge how I love Valentine
   Whose life's as tender° to me as my soul!
   And full as much, for more there cannot be,
   I do detest false perjured Proteus.
   Therefore be gone; solicit me no more.   40

Proteus. What dangerous action, stood it next to death,
   Would I not undergo for one calm look!
   O' tis the curse in love, and still approved,°
   When women cannot love where they're beloved!

Silvia. When Proteus cannot love where he's beloved!   45
   Read over Julia's heart, thy first, best love,
   For whose dear sake thou didst then rend thy faith
   Into a thousand oaths; and all those oaths
   Descended into perjury, to love me.
   Thou hast no faith left now, unless thou'dst two,   50
   And that's far worse than none; better have none
   Than plural faith, which is too much by one.
   Thou counterfeit to thy true friend!

37 *tender* precious   43 *still approved* perennially proved true

Proteus.   In love,
Who respects friend?

Silvia.   All men but Proteus.

55 *Proteus.* Nay, if the gentle spirit of moving words
Can no way change you to a milder form,
I'll woo you like a soldier, at arms' end,
And love you 'gainst the nature of love—force ye.

Silvia. O heaven!

Proteus.   I'll force thee yield to my desire.

Valentine. [*Advancing*] Ruffian, let go that rude uncivil
60   touch,
Thou friend of an ill fashion!°

Proteus.   Valentine!

Valentine. Thou common° friend, that's without faith
or love—
For such is a friend now; treacherous man!
Thou hast beguiled my hopes; nought but mine eye
65   Could have persuaded me. Now I dare not say
I have one friend alive; thou wouldst disprove me.
Who should be trusted, when one's right hand
Is perjured to the bosom? Proteus,
I am sorry I must never trust thee more,
70   But count the world a stranger for thy sake.
The private° wound is deepest. O time most accurst,
'Mongst all foes that a friend should be the worst!

Proteus. My shame and guilt confounds° me.
Forgive me, Valentine. If hearty sorrow
75   Be a sufficient ransom for offense,
I tender't here; I do as truly suffer
As e'er I did commit.°

Valentine.   Then I am paid;°

---

61 *friend of an ill fashion* i.e., false friend   62 *common* i.e.,
no better than the ordinary   71 *private* intimate (here, given by
a friend)   73 *confounds* destroys   76–77 *I do . . . did commit* i.e.,
I do indeed suffer, as truly as I did commit the fault   77 *paid*
satisfied

And once again I do receive thee honest.°
Who by repentance is not satisfied
Is nor of heaven nor earth, for these are pleased.   80
By penitence th' Eternal's wrath's appeased;
And, that my love may appear plain and free,
All that was mine in Silvia I give thee.

Julia. O me unhappy!   [*Swoons.*]

Proteus. Look to the boy.   85

Valentine. Why, boy! Why, wag! How now! What's
the matter? Look up; speak.

Julia. O good sir, my master charged me to deliver a
ring to Madam Silvia, which, out of my neglect, was
never done.   90

Proteus. Where is that ring, boy?

Julia.   Here 'tis; this is it.

Proteus. How! Let me see.
Why, this is the ring I gave to Julia.

Julia. O, cry you mercy,° sir, I have mistook.
This is the ring you sent to Silvia.   95

Proteus. But how cam'st thou by this ring? At my
depart I gave this unto Julia.

Julia. And Julia herself did give it me;
And Julia herself hath brought it hither.

Proteus. How! Julia!   100

Julia. Behold her that gave aim to° all thy oaths,
And entertained 'em deeply in her heart.
How oft hast thou with perjury cleft the root!
O Proteus, let this habit° make thee blush!
Be thou ashamed that I have took upon me   105
Such an immodest raiment, if shame live
In a disguise of love.°

78 *receive thee honest* accept you as being honorable   94 *cry you
mercy* I beg your pardon   101 *gave aim to* was the object (target)
of   104 *habit* i.e., her boy's garb   106–07 *if shame . . . of love*
if it can be shameful to disguise oneself for the sake of love

It is the lesser blot, modesty finds,
Women to change their shapes than men their
   minds.

Proteus. Than men their minds! 'Tis true. O heaven,
110   were man
But constant, he were perfect! That one error
Fills him with faults, makes him run through all th'
   sins:
Inconstancy falls off ere it begins.°
What is in Silvia's face, but I may spy
115   More fresh in Julia's with a constant eye?

Valentine. Come, come, a hand from either.
Let me be blest to make this happy close;°
'Twere pity two such friends should be long foes.

Proteus. Bear witness, Heaven, I have my wish forever.

120 *Julia.* And I mine.

[*Enter Outlaws, with Duke and Thurio.*]

Outlaws. A prize, a prize, a prize!

Valentine. Forbear, forbear, I say! It is my lord the
   Duke.
Your Grace is welcome to a man disgraced,
Banished Valentine.

Duke.   Sir Valentine!

125 *Thurio.* Yonder is Silvia, and Silvia's mine.

Valentine. Thurio, give back,° or else embrace thy
   death.
Come not within the measure° of my wrath.
Do not name Silvia thine; if once again,
Verona° shall not hold thee. Here she stands.
130   Take but possession of her with a touch:
I dare thee but to breathe upon my love.

---

113 *Inconstancy . . . begins* i.e., the inconstant man proves false
even before he begins to love   117 *close* joining of hands   126
give back back off   127 *measure* range, reach   129 *Verona* (i.e.,
Milan; see III.i.81,n.)

Thurio. Sir Valentine, I care not for her, I.
 I hold him but a fool that will endanger
 His body for a girl that loves him not.
 I claim her not, and therefore she is thine.   *135*

Duke. The more degenerate and base art thou,
 To make such means for° her as thou hast done,
 And leave her on such slight conditions.
 Now, by the honor of my ancestry,
 I do applaud thy spirit, Valentine,   *140*
 And think thee worthy of an empress' love.
 Know, then, I here forget all former griefs,
 Cancel all grudge, repeal° thee home again,
 Plead a new state in thy unrivaled merit,°
 To which I thus subscribe: Sir Valentine,   *145*
 Thou art a gentleman, and well derived;
 Take thou thy Silvia, for thou hast deserved her.

Valentine. I thank your Grace; the gift hath made me
  happy.
 I now beseech you, for your daughter's sake,
 To grant one boon that I shall ask of you.   *150*

Duke. I grant it, for thine own, whate'er it be.

Valentine. These banished men that I have kept withal°
 Are men endued° with worthy qualities.
 Forgive them what they have committed here,
 And let them be recalled from their exile: *155*
 They are reformèd, civil, full of good,
 And fit for great employment, worthy lord.

Duke. Thou hast prevailed; I pardon them and thee.
 Dispose of them as thou know'st their deserts.
 Come, let us go. We will include all jars°   *160*
 With triumphs, mirth, and rare solemnity.°

137 *means for* efforts to win   143 *repeal* recall (from banishment)   144 *plead . . . merit* (the general sense appears to be one of the following: (1) plead to be restored to your good graces, having formerly misjudged them (2) proclaim that you are elevated to a new place in my favor, earned by your unrivaled merit)   152 *kept withal* lived with   153 *endued* endowed   160 *include all jars* conclude all discords   161 *triumphs . . . solemnity* celebrations . . . festivity

Valentine. And, as we walk along, I dare be bold
  With our discourse to make your Grace to smile.
  What think you of this page, my lord?

165 *Duke*. I think the boy hath grace in him; he blushes.

Valentine. I warrant you, my lord, more grace than
  boy.

Duke. What mean you by that saying?

Valentine. Please you, I'll tell you as we pass along,
  That you will wonder what hath fortunèd.°
170 Come, Proteus; 'tis your penance but° to hear
  The story of your loves discoverèd.°
  That done, our day of marriage shall be yours;
  One feast, one house, one mutual happiness.

                                        Exeunt.

                      FINIS

----

169 *fortunèd* chanced   170 *'tis your penance but* your only penance
is   171 *discoverèd* revealed

Textual Note

The Two Gentlemen of Verona was first printed in the First Folio of 1623, which is the authority for the present text. In the Folio it is the second play, standing between *The Tempest* and *The Merry Wives of Windsor,* the title of the latter play mistakenly appearing at the top of the final two pages. Names of characters who participate in each scene are grouped at the head of the scene, without notice made of the point of their entrance. The present edition deletes these names, and provides them, in square brackets, at the appropriate places later in the scenes. The Folio gives "Protheus" for "Proteus" and places the dramatis personae at the end of the text. Certain irregularities occur in place names, as though Shakespeare had changed his mind or become confused about principal locations; thus in II.v Padua rather than Milan is identified as the place of action by Speed, and in III.i the Duke of Milan speaks of a lady "in Verona here." In the present edition, speech prefixes have been regularized, spelling and punctuation have been modernized, and obvious typographical errors have been corrected. Added material (stage directions, etc.) is set in brackets. Act and scene divisions are those of the Folio, translated from Latin into English. The relatively few emendations of the Folio text are indicated below: the present reading is given in italics, followed by the Folio reading in roman.

I.i.65 *leave* loue   77 *a sheep* Sheepe   144–45 *testerned* œstern'd

I.ii.88 *your* you

I.iii.91 *Exeunt* Exeunt. Finis

II.iii.29 *wood* would

II.iv.49 *father's in* father is in   107 *mistress* a Mistresse   165 *makes* make   195 *Is it mine eye* It is mine   213 *Exit* Exeunt

II.v.38 *that my* that that my

III.i.281 *master's ship* Mastership   318 *kissed fasting* fasting 378 s.d. *Exit* Exeunt

IV.i.10 *he's* he is   35 *miserable* often miserable   49 *An* And 49 *near* Neece

IV.ii.111 *his* her

IV.iii.18 *abhors* abhor'd

IV.iv.70 *thou* thee   74 *to leave* not leaue   205 *Exit* Exeunt

V.ii.18 *your peace* you peace   32 *Sir Eglamour* Eglamoure   56 *Exit* Exeunt

The Source of
The Two Gentlemen of Verona

Both because its plot is filled with well-known romance elements and because its poetic style is laden with rhetorical devices fashionable at the time it was written, *The Two Gentlemen of Verona* appears inevitably to owe an unusual number of debts to a wide variety of materials. In its conventions as well as in its basic materials and their manner of use, it is as deeply embedded in the literary life of its time as any work of Shakespeare's.

The central theme of the play—conflict between the duties of friendship and love—had been used by Boccaccio in *La Teseide,* by Chaucer in *The Knight's Tale,* and by Lyly in *Euphues: The Anatomy of Wit* and *Endimion;* but, indeed, this theme is ancient and widespread, and Shakespeare would have encountered it in any event. Specific incidents and motifs in the play, such as Julia's disguise as a boy, may have been suggested by Sidney's pastoral romance of *Arcadia;* the abrupt election of Valentine as captain of the outlaws may derive from the same source. Many echoes of Brooke's *Romeus and Juliet,* the narrative poem which Shakespeare followed in *Romeo and Juliet,* occur in the play, perhaps the most notable being the device of the rope ladder which figures prominently in both plays.

In poetic manner and attitude, the play shows the pervasive influence of Lyly, the fashionable stylist of courtly language and the master of dramatic artifice in dialogue, scene, and character. Long stretches of wit duels between servant and servant, servant and master, lady and attendant, filled with quips and quirks and turns of phrase, mark the play as Lylyan in its most basic conception. In *The Two Gentlemen of Verona* the artifices of Lyly are more than superficial ornamentation; they are organic.

For the core of the play, however, which is the love story of Julia and Proteus, Shakespeare went to a prose romance originally written in Spanish, the *Diana Enamorada,* by the Portuguese Jorge de Montemayor, published in 1542. How Shakespeare came to know this work is uncertain, for though it was translated into English by Bartholomew Yonge about 1582, the translation was not published until 1598—some four to six years after the play was written. It has been suggested that Shakespeare could have become acquainted with the *Diana* through a French translation made before 1590; that he may have seen Yonge's manuscript before it was published; or that the story was represented in a play now lost.

In any event, it is now generally accepted that Montemayor's romance somehow came to serve as Shakespeare's principal source, and, accordingly, an abridged version of the story follows. Inserted references to acts and scenes mark incidents of special interest.

Jorge de Montemayor

from *Diana Enamorada*

You shall therefore know, fair nymphs, that great Vandalia is my native country, a province not far hence, where I was born, in a city called Soldina, my mother called Delia, my father Andronius, for lineage and possessions the chiefest of all that province. It fell out that as my

Translated by Bartholomew Yonge, 1598

mother was married many years and had no children (by reason whereof she lived so sad and malcontent that she enjoyed not one merry day), with tears and sighs she daily importuned the heavens, and with a thousand vows and devout offerings besought God to grant her the sum of her desire: whose omnipotency it pleased, beholding from his imperial throne her continual orisons, to make her barren body (the greater part of her age being now spent and gone) to become fruitful. What infinite joy she conceived thereof, let her judge, that after a long desire of anything, fortune at last doth put it into her hands. Of which content my father Andronius being no less partaker, showed such tokens of inward joy as are impossible to be expressed. My mother Delia was so much given to reading of ancient histories that if, by reason of sickness or any important business, she had not been hindered, she would never (by her will) have passed the time away in any other delight; who (as I said) being now with child and finding herself on a night ill at ease, entreated my father to read something unto her, that her mind being occupied in contemplation thereof, she might the better pass her grief away. My father, who studied for nothing else but to please her in all he might, began to read unto her the history of Paris, when the three ladies referred their proud contention for the golden apple to his conclusion and judgment. But as my mother held it for an infallible opinion that Paris had partially given that sentence (persuaded thereunto by a blind passion of beauty), so she said, that without all doubt he did not with due reason and wisdom consider the goddess of battles; for, as martial and heroical feats (said she) excelled all other qualities, so with equity and justice the apple should have been given to her. My father answered that since the apple was to be given to the fairest, and that Venus was fairer than any of the rest, Paris had rightly given his judgment, if that harm had not ensued thereof, which afterwards did. To this my mother replied that, though it was written in the apple that it should be given to the fairest, it was not to be understood of corporal beauty, but of the intellectual beauty of the mind. And therefore since fortitude was a thing that made one most beautiful, and the exercise of arms an exterior act of this virtue, she affirmed that to the goddess of battles this apple should be given, if Paris had judged like a prudent and unappassionate judge. So that, fair nymphs, they spent a great part of the night in this controversy, both of them alleging the most reasons they could to confirm their own purpose. They persisting in this point, sleep began to overcome her whom the reasons and arguments of her husband could not once move; so that being very deep in her disputations, she fell into as deep a sleep, to whom (my father being now gone to his chamber) appeared the goddess Venus, with as frowning a countenance as fair, and said, "I marvel, Delia, who hath moved thee to be so contrary to her that was never opposite to thee? If thou hadst but called to mind the time when thou wert so overcome in love for Andronius, thou wouldest not have paid me the debt thou owest me with so ill coin. But thou shalt not escape free from my due anger; for thou shalt bring forth a son and a daughter, whose birth shall cost thee no less than thy life, and them their contentment, for uttering so much in disgrace of my honor and beauty: both which shall be as unfortunate in their love as any were ever in all their lives, or to the age wherein, with remediless sighs, they shall breathe forth the sum of their ceaseless sorrows." And having said thus, she vanished away: when, likewise, it seemed to my mother that the goddess Pallas came to her in a vision, and with a merry countenance said thus unto her: "With what sufficient rewards may I be able to requite the due regard, most happy and discreet Delia, which thou hast alleged in my favor against thy husband's obstinate opinion, except it be by making thee understand that thou shalt bring forth a son and a daughter, the most fortunate in arms that have been to their times." Having thus said, she vanished out of her sight, and my mother, through exceeding fear, awaked immediately. Who, within a month after, at one birth was delivered of me and of a brother of mine, and died in childbed, leaving my father the most sorrowful man in the world for her sudden death; for grief whereof, within a little while after, he also died. And because you may know, fair nymphs, in what great extremities love hath put me, you must understand that (being a woman of that quality and disposition as you have heard) I have been forced by my cruel destiny to leave my natural habit and liberty, and the due respect of mine honor, to follow him who thinks (perhaps) that I do but lose it by loving him so extremely. Behold how bootless and unseemly it is for a woman to be so dextrous in arms, as if it were her proper nature and kind, wherewith, fair nymphs, I had never been indued, but that, by means thereof, I should come to do you this little service against these villainies; which I account no less than if fortune had begun to satisfy in part some of those infinite wrongs that she hath continually done me. The nymphs were so amazed at her words that they could neither ask nor answer anything to that the fair shepherdess told them, who, prosecuting her history, said:

My brother and I were brought up in a nunnery, where an aunt of ours was abbess, until we had accomplished twelve years of age, at what time we were taken from thence again, and my brother was carried to the mighty and invincible King of Portugal his court (whose noble fame and princely liberality was bruited over all the world) where, being grown to years able to manage arms, he achieved as valiant and almost incredible enterprises by them as he suffered unfortunate disgraces and foils by love. And with all this he was so highly favored of that magnificent king that he would never suffer him to depart from his court. Unfortunate I, reserved by my sinister destinies to greater mishaps, was carried to a grandmother of mine, which place I would I had never seen, since it was an occasion of such a sorrowful life as never any woman suffered the like. And because there is not anything, fair nymphs, which I am not forced to tell you, as well for the great virtue and deserts which your excellent beauties do testify, as also for that for my mind doth give me, that you shall be no small part and means of my comfort, know that as I was in my grandmother's house, and almost seventeen years old, a certain young gentleman fell in love with me, who dwelt no further from our house than the length of a garden terrace, so that he might see me every summer's night when I walked in the garden. Whenas therefore ingrateful Felix had beheld in that place the unfortunate Felismena (for this is the name of the woeful woman that tells you her mishaps) he was extremely enamored of me, or else did cunningly dissemble it, I not knowing then whether of these two I might believe, but am now assured that whosoever believes least, or nothing at all in these affairs, shall be most at ease. Many days Don Felix spent in endeavoring to make me know the pains which he suffered for me, and many more did I spend in making the matter strange, and that he did not suffer them for my sake. And I know not why love delayed the time so long by forcing me to love him, but only that (when he came indeed) he might enter into my heart at once, and with greater force and violence. [I.i] When he had, therefore, by sundry signs, as by tilt and tourneys, and by prancing up and down upon his proud jennet before my windows, made it manifest that he was in love with me (for at the first I did not so well perceive it) he determined in the end to write a letter unto me; and having practiced divers times before with a maid of mine, and at length, with many gifts and fair promises, gotten her good will and furtherance, he gave her the letter to deliver to me. [I.ii] But to see the means that Rosina made unto me (for so was she called), the dutiful services and unwonted circumstances, before she did deliver it, the oaths that she sware unto me, and the subtle words and serious protestations she used, it was a pleasant thing, and worthy the noting. To whom (nevertheless) with an angry countenance I turned again, saying, "If I had not regard of mine own estate, and what hereafter might be said, I would make this shameless face of thine be known ever after for a mark of an impudent and bold minion: but because it is the first time, let this suffice that I have said and give thee warning to take heed of the second."

Methinks I see now the crafty wench, how she held her peace, dissembling very cunningly the sorrow that she conceived by my angry answer; for she feigned a counterfeit smiling, saying, "Jesus, Mistress! I gave it you, because you might laugh at it, and not to move your patience with it in this sort; for if I had any thought that it would have provoked you to anger, I pray God He may show His wrath as great towards me as ever He did to the daughter of any mother." And with this she added many words more (as she could do well enough) to pacify the feigned anger and ill opinion that I had conceived of her, and taking her letter with her, she departed from me. This having passed thus, I began to imagine what might ensue thereof, and love (methought) did put a certain desire into my mind to see the letter, though modesty and shame forbade me to ask it of my maid, especially for the words that had passed between us, as you have heard. And so I continued all that day until night, in variety of many thoughts; but when Rosina came to help me to bed, God knows how desirous I was to have her entreat me again to take the letter, but she would never speak unto me about it, nor (as it seemed) did so much as once think thereof. Yet to try, if by giving her some occasion I might prevail, I said unto her: "And is it so, Rosina, that Don Felix, without any regard to mine honor, dares write unto me?" "These are things, mistress," said she demurely to me again, "that are commonly incident to love, wherefore I beseech you pardon me, for if I had thought to have angered you with it, I would have first pulled out the balls of mine eyes." How cold my heart was at that blow, God knows, yet did I dissemble the matter and suffer myself to remain that night only with my desire, and with occasion of little sleep. And so it was, indeed, for that (methought) was the longest and most painful night that ever I passed. But when, with a slower pace (than I desired) the wished day was come, the discreet and subtle Rosina came into my chamber to help me to make me ready, in doing whereof, of purpose she let the letter closely fall, which when I perceived, "What is that that fell down?" said I. "Let me see it." "It is nothing, mistress," said she. "Come, come, let me see it," said I. "What! Move me not, or else tell me what it is." "Good Lord, mistress," said she, "why will you see it: it is the letter I would have given you yesterday." "Nay, that it is

not," said I. "Wherefore show it me, that I may see if
you lie or no." I had no sooner said so but she put it into
my hands, saying, "God never give me good if it be any
other thing"; and although I knew it well indeed, yet I
said, "What, this is not the same, for I know that well
enough, but it is one of thy lover's letters: I will read it,
to see in what need he standeth of thy favor." And opening it, I found it contained this that followeth.

> I ever imagined, dear mistress, that your discretion and
> wisdom would have taken away the fear I had to write
> unto you, the same knowing well enough (without any
> letter at all) how much I love you, but the very same hath
> so cunningly dissembled that wherein I hoped the only
> remedy of my griefs had been, therein consisted my great-
> est harm. If according to your wisdom you censure my
> boldness, I shall not then (I know) enjoy one hour of
> life; but if you do consider of it according to love's ac-
> customed effects, then will I not exchange my hope for
> it. Be not offended, I beseech you, good lady, with my
> letter, and blame me not for writing unto you, until you
> see by experience whether I can leave off to write: and
> take me besides into the possession of that which is yours,
> since all is mine doth wholly consist in your hands, the
> which, with all reverence and dutiful affection, a thousand
> times I kiss.

When I had now seen my Don Felix his letter, whether
it was for reading it at such a time, when by the same
he showed that he loved me more than himself, or whether
he had disposition and regiment over part of this wearied
soul to imprint that love in it whereof he wrote unto me,
I began to love him too well (and, alas, for my harm!),
since he was the cause of so much sorrow as I have passed
for his sake. Whereupon, asking Rosina forgiveness of
what was past (as a thing needful for that which was to
come) and committing the secrecy of my love to her fidelity, I read the letter once again, pausing a little at every
word (and a very little indeed it was), because I concluded
so soon with myself to do that I did, although in very

truth it lay not otherwise in my power to do. Wherefore, calling for paper and ink, I answered his letter thus.

Esteem not so slightly of mine honor, Don Felix, as with feigned words to think to inveigle it, or with thy vain pretenses to offend it any ways. I know well enough what manner of man thou art, and how great thy desert and presumption is; from whence thy boldness doth arise (I guess), and not from the force (which thing thou wouldst fain persuade me) of thy fervent love. And if it be so (as my suspicion suggesteth) thy labor is as vain as thy imagination presumptuous, by thinking to make me do anything contrary to that which I owe unto mine honor. Consider (I beseech thee) how seldom things commenced under subtlety and dissimulation have good success; and that it is not the part of a gentleman to mean them one way and speak them another. Thou prayest me (amongst other things) to admit thee into possession of that that is mine: but I am of so ill an humor in matters of this quality, that I trust not things experienced, how much less then thy bare words; yet, nevertheless, I make no small account of that which thou hast manifested to me in thy letter; for it is enough that I am incredulous, though not unthankful.

This letter did I send, contrary to that I should have done, because it was the occasion of all my harms and griefs; for after this, he began to wax more bold by unfolding his thoughts and seeking out the means to have a parley with me. In the end, fair nymphs, a few days being spent in his demands and my answers, false love did work in me after his wonted fashions, every hour seizing more strongly upon my unfortunate soul. The tourneys were now renewed, the music by night did never cease; amorous letters and verses were recontinued on both sides; and thus passed I away almost a whole year, at the end whereof I felt myself so far in his love that I had no power to retire nor stay myself from disclosing my thoughts unto him, the thing which he desired more than his own life. [I.iii] But my adverse fortune afterwards would, that of

these our mutual loves (when as now they were most assured) his father had some intelligence, and whosoever
revealed them first persuaded him so cunningly that his
father (fearing lest he would have married me out of
hand) sent him to the great Princess Augusta Caesarina's
court, telling him it was not meet that a young gentleman,
and of so noble a house as he was, should spend his youth
idly at home, where nothing could be learned but exam-
ples of vice, whereof the very same idleness (he said) was
the only mistress. He went away so pensive that his great
grief would not suffer him to acquaint me with his departure; which when I knew, how sorrowful I remained,
she may imagine that hath been at any time tormented
with like passion. To tell you now the life that I led in his
absence, my sadness, sighs, and tears, which every day I
poured out of these wearied eyes, my tongue is far un-
able: if then my pains were such that I cannot now express them, how could I then suffer them? [II.vii] But
being in the midst of my mishaps, and in the depth of
those woes which the absence of Don Felix caused me
to feel, and it seeming to me that my grief was without
remedy, if he were once seen or known of the ladies in
that court (more beautiful and gracious than myself), by
occasion whereof, as also by absence (a capital enemy to
love) I might easily be forgotten, I determined to adventure that which I think never any woman imagined; which
was to apparel myself in the habit of a man and to hie
me to the court to see him in whose sight all my hope
and content remained. Which determination I no sooner
thought of than I put in practice, love blinding my eyes
and mind with an inconsiderate regard of mine own estate and condition. To the execution of which attempt I
wanted no industry; for, being furnished with the help of
one of my approved friends and treasuress of my secrets,
who bought me such apparel as I willed her, and a good
horse for my journey, I went not only out of my country
but out of my dear reputation, which (I think) I shall
never recover again; and so trotted directly to the court,
passing by the way many accidents, which (if time would
give me leave to tell them) would not make you laugh a

little to hear them. Twenty days I was in going thither, at the end of which, being come to the desired place, I took up mine inn in a street less frequented with concourse of people: and the great desire I had to see the destroyer of my joy did not suffer me to think of any other thing but how or where I might see him. To inquire of him of mine host I durst not, lest my coming might (perhaps) have been discovered; and to seek him forth I though it not best, lest some inopinate mishap might have fallen out, whereby I might have been known. Wherefore I passed all that day in these perplexities while night came on, each hour whereof (methought) was a whole year unto me. [IV.i] But midnight being a little past, mine host called at my chamber door and told me if I was desirous to hear some brave music I should arise quickly and open a window towards the street. The which I did by and by, and making no noise at all, I heard how Don Felix his page, called Fabius (whom I knew by his voice), said to others that came with him, "Now it is time, my masters, because the lady is in the gallery over her garden, taking the fresh air of the cool night." He had no sooner said so but they began to wind three cornets and a sackbut, with such skill and sweetness that it seemed celestial music; and then began a voice to sing, the sweetest (in my opinion) that ever I heard. And though I was in suspense by hearing Fabius speak, whereby a thousand doubts and imaginations (repugnant to my rest) occurred in my mind, yet I neglected not to hear what was sung, because their operations were not of such force that they were able to hinder the desire nor distemper the delight that I conceived by hearing it. That therefore which was sung were these verses:

> Sweet mistress, harken unto me,
>   (If it grieves thee to see me die)
> And hearing though it grieveth thee,
>   To hear me yet, do not deny.
>
> O grant me then this short content,
>   For forced I am to thee to fly:

My sighs do not make thee relent,
  Nor tears thy heart do mollify.

Nothing of mine doth give thee pain,
  Nor thou think'st of no remedy:
Mistress, how long shall I sustain
  Such ill as still thou dost apply?

In death there is no help, be sure,
  But in thy will, where it doth lie:
For all those ills which death doth cure,
  Alas, they are but light to try.

My troubles do not trouble thee,
  Nor hope to touch thy soul so nigh:
O! From a will that is so free,
  What should I hope when I do cry?

How can I mollify that brave
  And stony heart, of pity dry?
Yet mistress, turn those eyes (that have
  No peers) shining like stars in sky;

But turn them not in angry sort,
  If thou wilt not kill me thereby:
Though yet in anger, or in sport,
  Thou killest only with thine eye.

After they had first, with a concert of music, sung this
song, two played, the one upon a lute, the other upon a
silver-sounding harp, being accompanied with the sweet
voice of my Don Felix. The great joy that I felt in hearing him cannot be imagined, for (methought) I heard
him now as in that happy and passed time of our loves.
But after the deceit of this imagination was discovered,
seeing with mine eyes and hearing with mine ears that
this music was bestowed upon another and not on me,
God knows what a bitter death it was unto my soul: and
with a grievous sigh that carried almost my life away with
it, I asked mine host if he knew what the lady was for

whose sake the music was made? He answered me that he could not imagine on whom it was bestowed, because in that street dwelled many noble and fair ladies. And when I saw he could not satisfy my request, I bent mine ears again to hear my Don Felix, who now, to the tune of a delicate harp, whereon he sweetly played, began to sing this sonnet following:

A SONNET

My painful years impartial Love was spending
   In vain and bootless hopes my life appaying,
   And cruel Fortune to the world bewraying
Strange samples of my tears that have no ending.
Time everything to truth at last commending,
   Leaves of my steps such marks, that now betraying,
   And all deceitful trusts shall be decaying,
And none have cause to 'plain of his offending.
She, whom I loved to my obliged power,
   That in her sweetest love to me discovers
Which never yet I knew (those heavenly pleasures),
And I do say, exclaiming every hour,
   Do not you see what makes you wise, O lovers?
Love, Fortune, Time, and my fair mistress' treasures.

The sonnet being ended, they paused a while, playing on four lutes together, and on a pair of virginals, with such heavenly melody that the whole world (I think) could not afford sweeter music to the ear nor delight to any mind not subject to the pangs of such predominant grief and sorrow as mine was. But then four voices, passing well tuned and set together, began to sing this song following:

A SONG

That sweetest harm I do not blame,
   First caused by thy fairest eyes,
But grieve, because too late I came
   To know my fault, and to be wise.

I never knew a worser kind of life,
To live in fear, from boldness still to cease:
Nor worse than this, to live in such a strife,
Whether of both, to speak or hold my peace?

And so the harm I do not blame,
Caused by thee or thy fair eyes;
But that to see how late I came
To know my fault, and to be wise.

I ever more did fear that I should know
Some secret things and doubtful in their kind,
Because the surest things do ever go
Most contrary unto my wish and mind.

And yet by knowing of the same
There is no hurt; but it denies
My remedy, since late I came
To know my fault, and to be wise.

When this song was ended, they began to sound divers
sort of instruments and voices most excellently agreeing
together and with such sweetness that they could not
choose but delight any very much who were so far from
it as I. About dawning of the day the music ended, and
I did what I could to espy out my Don Felix, but the dark-
ness of the night was mine enemy therein. And seeing now
that they were gone, I went to bed again, where I bewailed
my great mishap, knowing that he whom most of all I
loved had so unworthily forgotten me, whereof his music
was too manifest a witness. And when it was time I arose
and, without any other consideration, went straight to the
princess her palace, where (I thought) I might see that
which I so greatly desired, determining to call myself
Valerius, if any (perhaps) did ask my name. Coming
therefore to a fair broad court before the palace gate, I
viewed the windows and galleries, where I saw such store
of blazing beauties and gallant ladies that I am not able
now to recount nor then to do any more but wonder at
their graces, their gorgeous attire, their jewels, their brave
fashions of apparel and ornaments wherewith they were

so richly set out. Up and down this place, before the windows, rode many lords and brave gentlemen in rich and sumptuous habits and mounted upon proud jennets, every one casting his eye to that part where his thoughts were secretly placed. God knows how greatly I desired to see Don Felix there, and that his injurious love had been in that famous palace; because I might then have been assured that he should never have got any other guerdon of his suits and services, but only to see and to be seen, and sometimes to speak to his mistress, whom he must serve before a thousand eyes, because the privilege of that place doth not give him any further leave. But it was my ill fortune that he had settled his love in that place where I might not be assured of this poor help. Thus, as I was standing near to the palace gate, I espied Fabius, Don Felix his page, coming in great haste to the palace, where, speaking a word or two with a porter that kept the second entry, he returned the same way he came. I guessed his errand was to know whether it were fit time for Don Felix to come to dispatch certain business that his father had in the court, and that he could not choose but come thither out of hand. And being in this supposed joy which his sight did promise me, I saw him coming along with a great train of followers attending on his person, all of them being bravely appareled in a livery of watchet silk, guarded with yellow velvet and stitched on either side with threads of twisted silver, wearing likewise blue, yellow, and white feathers in their hats. But my lord Don Felix had on a pair of ash-color hose, embroidered and drawn forth with watchet tissue; his doublet was of white satin, embroidered with knots of gold, and likewise an embroidered jerkin of the same colored velvet; and his short cape cloak was of black velvet, edged with gold lace, and hung full of buttons of pearl and gold and lined with a razed watchet satin: by his side he wore, at a pair of embroidered hangers, a rapier and dagger, with engraven hilts and pommel of beaten gold. On his head, a hat beset full of golden stars, in the midst of every which a rich orient pearl was enchased, and his feather was likewise blue, yellow, and white. Mounted he came upon a fair dapple gray jennet, with a rich furniture of blue, embroidered with gold and seed pearl. When I saw him in this rich equipage, I was so amazed at his sight that how extremely my senses were ravished with sudden joy I am not able, fair nymphs, to tell you. Truth it is that I could not but shed some tears for joy and grief, which his sight did make me feel, but, fearing to be noted by the standers-by, for that time I dried them up. But as Don Felix (being now come to the palace gate) was dismounted, and gone up a pair of stairs into the chamber of presence, I went to his men, where they were attending his return; and seeing Fabius, whom I had seen before amongst them, I took him aside and said unto him, "My friend, I pray you tell me what lord this is, which did but even now alight from his jennet, for (methinks) he is very like one whom I have seen before in another far country." Fabius then answered me thus: "Art thou such a novice in the court that thou knowest not Don Felix? I tell thee there is not any lord, knight, or gentleman better known in it than he." "No doubt of that," said I, "but I will tell thee what a novice I am and how small a time I have been in the court, for yesterday was the first that ever I came to it." "Nay then, I cannot blame thee," said Fabius, "if thou knowest him not. Know, then, that this gentleman is called Don Felix, born in Vandalia, and hath his chiefest house in the ancient city of Soldina, and is remaining in this court about certain affairs of his father's and his own." "But I pray you tell me," said I, "why he gives his liveries of these colors?" "If the cause were not so manifest, I would conceal it," said Fabius, "but since there is not any that knows it not and canst not come to any in this court who cannot tell thee the reason why, I think by telling thee it I do no more than in courtesy I am bound to do. Thou must therefore understand that he loves and serves a lady here in this city named Celia and therefore wears and gives for his livery an azure blue which is the color of the sky, and white and yellow, which are the colors of his lady and mistress." When I heard these words, imagine, fair nymphs, in what a plight I was; but dissembling my mishap and grief, I answered him: "This

lady certes is greatly beholding to him, because he thinks
not enough, by wearing her colors, to show how willing
he is to serve her, unless also he bear her name in his
livery; whereupon I guess she cannot but be very fair and
amiable." "She is no less, indeed," said Fabius, "although
the other whom he loved and served in our own country
in beauty far excelled this and loved and favored him
more than ever this did. But this mischievous absence doth
violate and dissolve those things which men think to be
most strong and firm." At these words, fair nymphs, was
I fain to come to some composition with my tears, which,
if I had not stopped from issuing forth, Fabius could not
have chosen but suspected, by the alteration of my countenance, that all was not well with me. And then the page
did ask me what countryman I was, my name and of
what calling and condition I was: whom I answered that
my country where I was born was Vandalia, my name
Valerius, and till that time served no master. "Then by
this reckoning," said he, "we are both countrymen and
may be both fellows in one house if thou wilt; for Don
Felix my master commanded me long since to seek him
out a page. Therefore if thou wilt serve him, say so. As
for meat, drink, and apparel, and a couple of shillings to
play away, thou shalt never want; besides pretty wenches,
which are not dainty in our street, as fair and amorous
as queens, of which there is not any that will not die for
the love of so proper a youth as thou art. And to tell
thee in secret (because, perhaps, we may be fellows), I
know where an old canon's maid is, a gallant fine girl,
whom if thou canst but find in thy heart to love and serve
as I do, thou shalt never want at her hands fine hand-
kerchers, pieces of bacon, and now and then wine of St.
Martin." When I heard this, I could not choose but laugh
to see how naturally the unhappy page played his part
by depainting forth their properties in their lively colors.
And because I thought nothing more commodious for my
rest, and for the enjoying of my desire, than to follow
Fabius his counsel, I answered him thus: "In truth, I
determined to serve none; but now, since fortune hath
offered me so good a service and at such a time, when I

am constrained to take this course of life, I shall not do amiss if I frame myself to the service of some lord or gentleman in this court, but especially of your master, because he seems to be a worthy gentleman, and such an one that makes more reckoning of his servants than another." "Ha, thou knowest him not so well as I," said Fabius, "for I promise thee, by the faith of a gentleman (for I am one indeed, for my father comes of the Cachopines of Laredo), that my master Don Felix is the best-natured gentleman that ever thou knewest in thy life, and one who useth his pages better than any other. And were it not for those troublesome loves, which makes us run up and down more and sleep less than we would, there were not such a master in the whole world again."

[IV.iv] In the end, fair nymphs, Fabius spake to his master Don Felix as soon as he was come forth, in my behalf, who commanded me the same night to come to him at his lodging. Thither I went, and he entertained me for his page, making the most of me in the world; where, being but a few days with him, I saw the messages, letters, and gifts that were brought and carried on both sides, grievous wounds (alas! and corr'sives to my dying heart), which made my soul to fly sometimes out of my body, and every hour in hazard to lose my forced patience before every one. But after one month was past, Don Felix began to like so well of me that he disclosed his whole love unto me from the beginning unto the present estate and forwardness that it was then in, committing the charge thereof to my secrecy and help; telling me that he was favored of her at the beginning and that afterwards she waxed weary of her loving and accustomed entertainment, the cause whereof was a secret report (whosoever it was that buzzed it into her ears) of the love that he did bear to a lady in his own country, and that his present love unto her was but to entertain the time while his business in the court were dispatched. "And there is no doubt," said Don Felix unto me, "but that, indeed, I did once commence that love that she lays to my charge; but God knows if now there be anything in the world that I love and esteem more dear and precious than her." When I heard him say so, you may imagine, fair nymphs, what a mortal dagger pierced my wounded heart. But with dissembling the matter the best I could, I answered him thus: "It were better, sir (methinks), that the gentlewoman should complain with cause, and that it were so indeed; for if the other lady, whom you served before, did not deserve to be forgotten of you, you do her (under correction, my lord) the greatest wrong in the world." "The love," said Don Felix again, "which I bear to my Celia will not let me understand it so; but I have done her (methinks) the greater injury, having placed my love first in another and not in her." "Of these wrongs," said I to myself, "I know who bears the worst away." And (disloyal) he, pulling a letter out of his bosom, which he had received the same hour from his mistress, read it into me, thinking he did me a great favor thereby, the contents whereof were these:

CELIA'S LETTER TO DON FELIX

Never anything that I suspected, touching thy love, hath been so far from the truth that hath not given me occasion to believe more often mine own imagination than thy innocence; wherein, if I do thee any wrong, refer it but to the censure of thine own folly. For well thou mightest have denied or not declared thy passed love, without giving me occasion to condemn thee by thine own confession. Thou sayest I was the cause that made thee forget thy former love. Comfort thyself, for there shall not want another to make thee forget thy second. And assure thyself of this, Lord Don Felix, that there is not anything more unbeseeming a gentleman than to find an occasion in a gentlewoman to lose himself for her love. I will say no more, but that in an ill, where there is no remedy, the best is not to seek out any.

After he had made an end of reading the letter, he said unto me, "What thinkest thou, Valerius, of these words?" "With pardon be it spoken, my lord, that your deeds are showed by them." "Go to," said Don Felix, "and speak no more of that." "Sir," said I, "they must like me well if they like you, because none can judge better of their words that love well than they themselves. But that which I think of the letter is that this gentlewoman would have been the first, and that Fortune had entreated her in such sort that all others might have envied her estate." "But what wouldest thou counsel me?" said Don Felix. "If thy grief doth suffer any counsel," said I, "that thy thoughts be divided into this second passion, since there is so much due to the first." Don Felix answered me again, sighing and knocking me gently on the shoulder, saying, "How wise art thou, Valerius, and what good counsel dost thou give me if I could follow it. Let us now go in to dinner, for when I have dined I will have thee carry me a letter to my lady Celia, and then thou shalt see if any other love is not worthy to be forgotten in lieu of thinking only of her." These were words that grieved Felismena to the heart, but because she had him before her eyes, whom she loved more than herself, the content that she had by only seeing him was a sufficient remedy of the pain that the greatest of these stings did make her feel. After Don Felix had dined, he called me unto him, and giving me a special charge what I should do (because he had imparted his grief unto me, and put his hope and remedy in my hands), he willed me to carry a letter to Celia, which he had already written, and reading it first unto me, it said thus:

DON FELIX HIS LETTER TO CELIA

The thought that seeks an occasion to forget the thing which it doth love and desire, suffers itself so easily to be known that (without troubling the mind much) it may be quickly discerned. And think not, fair lady, that I seek a remedy to excuse you of that wherewith it pleased you to use me, since I never came to be so much in credit with you that in lesser things I would do it. I have confessed unto you that indeed I once loved well, because that true love, without dissimulation, doth not suffer anything to be hid, and you, dear lady, make that an occasion to forget me, which should be rather a motive to love me better. I cannot persuade me that you make so small an account of yourself to think that I can forget you for anything that is, or hath ever been, but rather imagine that you write clean contrary to that which you have tried by my zealous love and faith towards you. Touching all those things that, in prejudice of my good will towards you, it pleaseth you to imagine, my innocent thoughts assure me to the contrary, which shall suffice to be ill recompensed besides being so ill thought of as they are.

After Don Felix had read this letter unto me, he asked me if the answer was correspondent to those words that his lady Celia had sent him in hers, and if there was anything therein that might be amended; whereunto I answered thus: "I think, sir, it is needless to amend this letter, or to make the gentlewoman amends to whom it is sent, but her whom you do injury so much with it. Which under your lordship's pardon I speak, because I am so much affected to the first love in all my life that there is not anything that can make me alter my mind." "Thou hast the greatest reason in the world," said Don Felix, "if I could persuade myself to leave off that which I have begun. But what wilt thou have me do, since absence hath frozen the former love, and the continual presence of a peerless beauty rekindled another more hot and fervent in me?" "Thus may she think herself," said I again, "unjustly deceived, whom first you loved, because that love which is subject to the power of absence cannot be termed love, and none can persuade me that it hath been love." These words did I dissemble the best I could, because I felt so sensible grief to see myself forgotten of him who had so great reason to love me, and whom I did love so much that I did more than any would have thought to make myself still unknown. But taking the letter and mine errand with me, I went to Celia's house, imagining by the way the woeful estate whereunto my hapless love had brought me; since I was forced to make war against mine own self, and to be the intercessor of a thing so contrary to mine own content. But coming to Celia's house, and finding a page standing at the door, I asked him if I might speak with his lady: who being informed of me from whence I came, told Celia how I would speak with her, commending therewithal my beauty and person unto her, and telling her besides that Don Felix had but lately entertained me into his service; which made Celia say unto him, "What, Don Felix so soon disclose his secret loves to a page, but newly entertained? He hath (belike) some great occasion that moves him to do it. Bid him come in, and let us know what he would have." In I came, and to the place where the enemy of my life was, and with great reverence kissing her hands, I delivered Don Felix his letter unto her. Celia took it and, casting her eyes upon me, I might perceive how my sight had made a sudden alteration in her countenance, for she was so far besides herself that for a good while she was not able to speak a word, but remembering herself at last, she said unto me, "What good fortune hath been so favorable to Don Felix to bring thee to this court, to make thee his page?" "Even that, fair lady," said I, "which is better than ever I imagined, because it hath been an occasion to make me behold such singular beauty and perfections as now I see clearly before mine eyes. And if the pains, the tears, the sighs, and the continual disquiets that my lord Don Felix hath suffered have grieved me heretofore, now that I have seen the source from whence they flow and the cause of all his ill, the pity that I had on him is now wholly converted into a certain kind of envy. But if it be true, fair lady, that my coming is welcome unto you, I beseech you by that which you owe to the great love which he bears you, that your answer may import no less unto him." "There is not anything," said Celia, "that I would not do for thee, though I were determined not to love him at all, who for my sake hath forsaken another. For it is no small point of wisdom for me to learn by other women's harms to be more wise and wary in mine own." "Believe not, good lady," said I, "that there is anything in the world that can make Don Felix forget you. And if he hath cast off another for your sake, wonder not thereat, when your beauty and wisdom is so great and the other's so small that there is no reason to think that he will (though he hath worthily forsaken her for your sake) or ever can forget you for any woman else in the world." "Dost thou then know Felismena," said Celia, "the lady whom thy master did once love and serve in his own country?" "I know her," said I, "although not so well as it was needful for me to have prevented so many mishaps" (and this I spake softly to myself). "For my father's house was near to hers; but seeing your great beauty adorned with such perfections and wisdom, Don Felix cannot be blamed if he hath forgotten his first love only to embrace and honor yours." To this did Celia answer, merrily and smiling, "Thou hast learned quickly of thy master to soothe." "Not so, fair lady," said I, "but to serve you would I fain learn: for flattery cannot be where (in the judgment of all) there are so manifest signs and proofs of this due commendation." Celia began in good earnest to ask me what manner of woman Felismena was, whom I answered that, touching her beauty, some thought her to be very fair; but I was never of that opinion, because she hath many days since wanted the chiefest thing that is requisite for it. "What is that?" said Celia. "Content of mind," said I, "because perfect beauty can never be, where the same is not adjoined to it." "Thou hast the greatest reason in the world," said she, "but I have seen some ladies whose lively hue sadness hath not one whit abated, and others whose beauty anger hath increased, which is a strange thing methinks." "Hapless is that beauty," said I, "that hath sorrow and anger the preservers and mistresses of it, but I cannot skill of these impertinent things. And yet that woman that must needs be molested with continual pain and trouble, with grief and care of mind and with other passions to make her look well, cannot be reckoned among the number of fair women, and for mine own part I do not account her so." "Wherein thou hast great reason," said she, "as in all things else that thou hast said, thou hast showed thyself wise and discreet." "Which I have dearly bought," said I again. "But I beseech you, gracious lady, to answer this letter, because my lord Don Felix may also have some contentment, by receiving this first well-employed service at my hands." "I am content," said Celia, "but first thou

must tell me if Felismena in matters of discretion be wise
and well advised?" "There was never any woman," said
I again, "more wise than she, because she hath been long
since beaten to it by her great mishaps; but she did never
advise herself well, for if she had (as she was accounted
wise) she had never come to have been so contrary to
herself." "Thou speakest so wisely in all thy answers,"
said Celia, "that there is not any that would not take great
delight to hear them." "Which are not viands," said I, "for
such a dainty taste, nor reasons for so ingenious and fine
a conceit, fair lady, as you have, but boldly affirming that
by the same I mean no harm at all." "There is not anything," said Celia, "whereunto thy wit cannot attain, but
because thou shalt not spend thy time so ill in praising
me, as thy master doth in praying me, I will read thy
letter and tell thee what thou shalt say unto him from
me." Whereupon unfolding it, she began to read it to
herself, to whose countenance and gestures in reading of
the same, which are oftentimes outward signs of the inward disposition and meaning of the heart, I gave a watchful eye. And when she had read it, she said unto me, "Tell
thy master that he that can so well by words express what
he means, cannot choose but mean as well as he saith,"
and coming nearer to me, she said softly in mine ear, "and
this for the love of thee, Valerius, and not so much for
Don Felix thy master his sake, for I see how much thou
lovest and tenderest his estate." "And from thence, alas,"
said I to myself, "did all my woes arise." Whereupon
kissing her hands for the great courtesy and favor she
showed me, I hied me to Don Felix with this answer,
which was no small joy to him to hear it, and another
death to me to report it, saying many times to myself
(when I did either bring him home some joyful tidings
or carry letters or tokens to her), "O thrice unfortunate
Felismena, that with thine own weapons art constrained
to wound thy ever-dying heart, and to heap up favors for
him who made so small account of thine." And so did I
pass away my life with so many torments of mind that
if by the sight of my Don Felix they had not been tem-
pered, it could not have otherwise been but that I must

needs have lost it. More than two months together did Celia hide from me the fervent love she bare me, although not in such sort but that by certain apparent signs I came to the knowledge thereof, which was no small lighting and ease of that grief which incessantly haunted my wearied spirits; for as I thought it a strong occasion, and the only mean to make her utterly forget Don Felix, so likewise I imagined that, perhaps, it might befall to him as it hath done to many that the force of ingratitude and contempt of his love might have utterly abolished such thoughts out of his heart. But, alas, it happened not so to my Don Felix; for the more he perceived that his lady forgot him, the more was his mind troubled with greater cares and grief, which made him lead the most sorrowful life that might be, whereof the least part did not fall to my lot. For remedy of whose sighs and piteous lamentations, poor Felismena (even by main force) did get favors from Celia, scoring them up (whensoever she sent them by me) in the catalogue of my infinite mishaps. For if by chance he sent her anything by any of his other servants, it was so slenderly accepted that he thought it best to send none unto her but myself, perceiving what inconvenience did ensue thereof. But God knows how many tears my messages cost me, and so many they were that in Celia's presence I ceased not to pour them forth, earnestly beseeching her with prayers and petitions not to entreat him so ill who loved her so much, because I would bind Don Felix to me by the greatest bond as never man in like was bound to any woman. My tears grieved Celia to the heart, as well for that I shed them in her presence, as also for that she saw if I meant to love her, I would not (for requital of hers to me) have solicited her with such diligence nor pleaded with such pity to get favors for another. And thus I lived in the greatest confusion that might be, amidst a thousand anxieties of mind, for I imagined with myself that if I made not a show that I loved her, as she did me, I did put it in hazard lest Celia, for despite of my simplicity or contempt, would have loved Don Felix more than before, and by loving him that mine could not have any good success; and if I feigned myself, on the other side, to be in love with her, it might have been an occasion to have made her reject my lord Don Felix, so that with the thought of his love neglected and with the force of her contempt, he might have lost his content, and after that, his life, the least of which two mischiefs to prevent I would have given a thousand lives, if I had them. Many days passed away in this sort, wherein I served him as a third between both, to the great cost of my contentment, at the end whereof the success of his love went on worse and worse, because the love that Celia did bear me was so great that the extreme force of her passion made her lose some part of that compassion she should have had of herself. And on a day after that I had carried and recarried many messages and tokens between them, sometimes feigning some myself from her unto him, because I could not see him (whom I loved so dearly) so sad and pensive, with many supplications and earnest prayers I besought Lady Celia with pity to regard the painful life that Don Felix passed for her sake, and to consider that by not favoring him she was repugnant to that which she owed to herself: which thing I entreated, because I saw him in such a case that there was no other thing to be expected of him but death, by reason of the continual and great pain which his grievous thoughts made him feel. But she with swelling tears in her eyes, and with many sighs, answered me thus: "Unfortunate and accursed Celia, that now in the end dost know how thou livest deceived with a false opinion of thy great simplicity (ungrateful Valerius) and of thy small discretion. I did not believe till now that thou didst crave favors of me for thy master, but only for thyself, and to enjoy my sight all that time that thou didst spend in suing to me for them. But now I see thou dost ask them in earnest, and that thou art so content to see me use him well, that thou canst not (without doubt) love me at all. O how ill dost thou acquit the love I bear thee, and that which, for thy sake, I do now forsake? O that time might revenge me of thy proud and foolish mind, since love hath not been the means to do it. For I cannot think that Fortune will be so contrary unto me, but that she will punish thee for contemning that great good which she meant to bestow on thee. And tell thy lord Don Felix that if he will see me alive, that he see me not at all: and thou, vile traitor, cruel enemy to my rest, come no more (I charge thee) before these wearied eyes, since their tears were never of force to make thee know how much thou art bound unto them." And with this she suddenly flang out of my sight with so many tears that mine were not of force to stay her. For in the greatest haste in the world she got her into her chamber where, locking the door after her, it availed me not to call and cry unto her, requesting with amorous and sweet words to open me the door and to take such satisfaction on me as it pleased her: nor to tell her many other things, whereby I declared unto her the small reason she had to be so angry with me and to shut me out. But with a strange kind of fury she said unto me, "Come no more, ungrateful and proud Valerius, in my sight, and speak no more unto me, for thou art not able to make satisfaction for such great disdain, and I will have no other remedy for the harm which thou hast done me, but death itself, the which with mine own hands I will take in satisfaction of that which thou deservest." Which words when I heard, I stayed no longer, but with a heavy cheer came to my Don Felix his lodging, and, with more sadness than I was able to dissemble, told him that I could not speak with Celia, because she was visited of certain gentlewomen her kinswomen. But the next day in the morning it was bruited over all the city that a certain trance had taken her that night, wherein she gave up the ghost, which struck all the court with no small wonder. But that which Don Felix felt by her sudden death, and how near it grieved his very soul, as I am not able to tell, so cannot human intendment conceive it, for the complaints he made, the tears, the burning sighs, and heartbreak sobs, were without all measure and number. But I say nothing of myself, when on the one side the unlucky death of Celia touched my soul very near, the tears of Don Felix on the other did cut my heart in two with grief: and yet this was nothing to that intolerable pain which afterwards I felt. For Don Felix heard no sooner of her death, but the same night he was missing in his house, that none of his servants nor anybody else could tell any news of him.

Whereupon you may perceive, fair nymphs, what cruel torments I did then feel: then did I wish a thousand times for death to prevent all these woes and miseries which afterwards befell unto me: for Fortune (it seemed) was but weary of those which she had but till then given me. But as all the care and diligence which I employed in seeking out my Don Felix was but in vain, so I resolved with myself to take this habit upon me as you see, wherein it is more than two years since I have wandered up and down, seeking him in many countries: but my Fortune hath denied me to find him out, although I am not a little now bound unto her by conducting me hither at this time, wherein I did you this small piece of service. Which, fair nymphs, believe me, I account (next after his life in whom I have put all my hope) the greatest content that might have fallen unto me. . . .

[There follows a discussion of the relationship of love to reason.]

The shepherdess having made an end of her sharp answer and Felismena beginning to arbitrate the matter between them, they heard a great noise in the other side of the meadow, like to the sound of blows and smiting of swords upon harness, as if some armed men had fought together, so that all of them with great haste ran to the place where they heard the noise, to see what the matter was. And being come somewhat near, they saw in a little island (which the river with a round turning had made) three knights fighting against one. And although he defended himself valiantly, by showing his approved strength and courage, yet the three knights gave him so much to do that he was fain to help himself by all the force and policy he could. They fought on foot, for their horses were tied to little trees that grew thereabout. And now by this time, the knight that fought all alone and defended himself had laid one of them at his feet with a blow of his good sword, which ended his life. But the other two that were very strong and valiant redoubled their force and blows so thick on him that he looked for no other thing than death. The shepherdess Felismena seeing the knight in so great danger, and if she did not speedily help him, that he could not escape with life, was not afraid to put hers in jeopardy by doing that which in such a case she thought she was bound to perform: wherefore putting a sharp-headed arrow into her bow, she said unto them: "Keep out, knights, for it is not beseeming men that make account of this name and honor, to take advantage of their enemies with so great odds." And aiming at the sight of one of their helmets, she burst it with such force that the arrow running into his eyes came out of the other side of his head so that he fell down dead to the ground. When the distressed knight saw two of his enemies dead, he ran upon the third with such force as if he had but then begun the combat; but Felismena helped him out of more trouble by putting another arrow into her bow, the which transpiercing his armor, she left under his left pap, and so justly smote his heart that this knight also followed his two companions. When the shepherds and the knight beheld what Felismena had done, and how at two shoots she had killed two such valiant knights, they were all in great wonder. The knight therefore, taking off his helmet and coming unto her, said: "How am I able, fair shepherdess, to requite so great a benefit and good turn as I have received at thy hands this day, but by acknowledging this debt forever in my grateful mind?" When Felismena beheld the knight's face and knew him, her senses were so troubled that being in such a trance she could scarce speak, but coming to herself again, she answered him: "Ah, my Don Felix, this is not the first debt wherein thou art bound unto me. And I cannot believe that thou wilt acknowledge this (as thou sayest) no more than thou hast done greater than this before. Behold to what a time and end my fortune and thy forgetness hath brought me, that she what was wont to be served of thee in the city with tilt and tourneys, and honored with many other things, whereby thou didst deceive me (or I suffered myself to be deceived), doth now wander up and down, exiled from her native country and liberty, for using thus thine own. If this brings thee not into the knowledge of that which thou owest me, remember how one whole year I served thee as thy page in the Princess Caesarina's court: and how I was a solicitor against myself, without discovering myself or my thoughts unto thee, but only to procure thy remedy and to help the grief which thine made thee feel. How many times did I get thee favors from thy mistress Celia to the great cost of my tears and griefs: all which account but small, Don Felix, in respect of those dangers (had they been unsufficient) wherein I would have spent my life for redress of thy pains, which thy injurious love afforded thee. And unless thou art weary of the great love that I have borne thee, consider and weigh with thyself the strange effects which the force of love hath caused me to pass. I went out of my native country and came to serve thee, to lament the ill that thou didst suffer, to take upon me the injuries and disgraces that I received therein; and to give thee any content, I cared not to lead the most bitter and painful life that ever woman lived. In the habit of a tender and dainty lady I loved thee more than thou canst imagine, and in the habit of a base page I served thee (a thing more contrary to my rest and reputation than I mean now to rehearse) and yet now in the habit of a poor and simple shepherdess I came to do thee this small service. What remains then more for me to do, but to sacrifice my life to thy loveless soul, if with the same yet I could give thee more content—and if in lieu thereof thou wouldest but remember how much I have loved and do yet love thee! Here hast thou thy sword in thy hand; let none therefore but thy self revenge the offense that I have done thee." When the knight heard Felismena's words and knew them all to be as true as he was disloyal, his heart by this strange and sudden accident recovered some force again to see what great injury he had done her, so that the thought thereof and the plenteous effusion of blood that issued out of his wounds made him like a dead man fall down in a swoon at fair Felismena's feet; who with great care and no less fear, laying his head in her lap, with showers of tears that rained from her eyes upon the knight's pale visage, began thus to lament: "What means this cruel Fortune? Is the period of my life come just with the last end of my Don Felix his days? Ah, my Don Felix (the cause of all my pain), if the plenteous tears, which for thy sake I have now shed, are not sufficient; and these which I now distill upon thy lovely cheeks, too few to make thee come to thyself again, what remedy shall this miserable soul have to prevent that this bitter joy by seeing thee turn not to occasion of utter despair. Ah, my Don Felix, awake my love, if thou dost but sleep or be'st in a trance, although I would not wonder if thou dost not, since never anything that I could do prevailed with thee to frame my least content." And in these and other lamentations was fair Felismena plunged, whom the Portugal shepherdesses with their tears and poor supplies endeavored to encourage, when on the sudden they saw a fair nymph coming over the stony causey that led the way into the island, with a golden bottle in one hand and a silver one in the other, whom Felismena knowing by and by, said unto her: "Ah, Doria, could any come at this time to succor me but thou, fair nymph? Come hither then, and thou shalt see the cause of all my troubles, the substance of my sighs, and the object of my thoughts, lying in the greatest danger of death that may be." "In like occurrents," said Doria, "virtue and a good heart most take place. Recall it then, fair Felismena, and revive thy daunted spirits, trouble not thyself any more, for now is the end of thy sorrows and the beginning of thy contentment come." And speaking these words, she besprinkled his face with a certain odoriferous water which she brought in the silver bottle, whereby he came to his memory again, and then said unto him: "If thou wilt recover thy life, sir knight, and give it her that hath passed such an ill one for thy sake, drink of the water in this bottle." The which Don Felix, taking in his hand, drunk a good draught and, resting upon it a little, found himself so whole of his wounds, which the three knights had given him, and of that which the love of Celia had made in his breast, that now he felt the pain no more which either of them had caused him than if he had never had them. And in this sort he began to rekindle the old love that he bore to Felismena, the which (he thought) was never more zealous than now. Whereupon sitting down upon the green grass, he took his lady and shepherdess by the hands and, kissing them many times, said thus unto her: "How small account would I make of my life, my dearest Felismena, for canceling that great bond wherein (with more than life) I am forever bound unto thee: for since I enjoy it by thy means, I think it no more than right to restore thee that which is thine own. . . . What words are sufficient to excuse the faults that I have committed against thy faith and firmest love and loyalty? . . . Truth is that I loved Celia well and forgot thee, but in such sort that thy wisdom and beauty did ever slide out of my mind. And the best is that I know not wherein to put this fault that may be so justly attributed to me; for if I will impute it to the young age that I was then in, since I had it to love thee, I should not have wanted it to have been firm in the faith that I owed thee. If to Celia's beauty it is clear that thine did far excel hers and all the world's besides. If to the change of time, this should have been the touchstone which should have showed the force and virtue of my firmness. If to injurious and traitorous absence, it serves as little for my excuse, since the desire of seeing thee should not have been absent from supporting thy image in my memory. Behold then, Felismena, what assured trust I put in thy goodness, that (without any other means) I dare put before thee the small reason thou hast to pardon me. But what shall I do to purchase pardon at thy gracious hands, or after thou hast pardoned me, to believe that thou art satisfied: for one thing grieves me more than anything else in the world, and this it is. That, though the love which thou hast borne me, and wherewith thou dost yet bless me, is an occasion (perhaps) to make thee forgive me and forget so many faults: yet I shall never lift up mine eyes to behold thee, but that every injury which I have done thee will be worse than a mortal incision in my guilty heart." The shepherdess Felismena, who saw Don Felix so penitent for his passed misdeeds and so affectionately returned to his first thoughts, with many tears told him that she did pardon him, because the love that she had ever borne him would suffer her to do no less: which if she had not thought to do, she would never have taken so great pains and so many weary journeys to seek him out, and many other things, wherewith Don Felix was confirmed in his former love. . . . And Don Felix wondered not a little to understand how his lady Felismena had served him so many days as his page, and that he was so far gone out of his wits and memory that he knew her not for all that while. And his joy on the other side to see that his lady loved him so well, was so great that by no means he could hide it. Thus therefore, riding on their way, they came to Diana's temple, where the sage Felicia was looking for their coming: and likewise the shepherd Arsileus, and Belisa, Sylvanus, and Selvagia, who were now come thither not many days before. They were welcomed on every side and with great joy entertained; but fair Felismena especially, who for her rare virtues and singular beauty was greatly honored of them all. There they were all married with great joy, feasts, and triumphs, which were made by all the goodly nymphs and by the sage and noble lady Felicia. . . .

Commentaries

SAMUEL JOHNSON

from *The Plays of William Shakespeare*

In this play there is a strange mixture of knowledge and ignorance, of care and negligence. The versification is often excellent, the allusions are learned and just; but the author conveys his heroes by sea from one inland town to another in the same country; he places the Emperor at Milan and sends his young men to attend him, but never mentions him more; he makes Proteus, after an interview with Silvia, say he has only seen her picture; and, if we may credit the old copies, he has, by mistaking places, left his scenery inextricable. The reason of all this confusion seems to be that he took his story from a novel, which he sometimes followed and sometimes forsook, sometimes remembered and sometimes forgot.

From *The Plays of William Shakespeare*, edited by Samuel Johnson. Vol. I. London: Printed for H. Woodfall, etc., 1768.

WILLIAM HAZLITT

from *Characters of Shakespear's Plays*

This is little more than the first outlines of a comedy loosely sketched in. It is the story of a novel dramatized with very little labor or pretension; yet there are passages of high poetical spirit, and of inimitable quaintness of humor, which are undoubtedly Shakespear's, and there is throughout the conduct of the fable a careless grace and felicity which marks it for his. One of the editors (we believe, Mr. Pope) remarks in a marginal note to *The Two Gentlemen of Verona*: "It is observable (I know not for what cause) that the style of this comedy is less figurative, and more natural and unaffected than the greater part of this author's, though supposed to be one of the first he wrote." Yet so little does the editor appear to have made up his mind upon this subject, that we find the following note to the very next (the second) scene. "This whole scene, like many others in these plays (some of which I believe were written by Shakespear, and others interpolated by the players) is composed of the lowest and most trifling conceits, to be accounted for only by the gross taste of the

From *Characters of Shakespear's Plays* by William Hazlitt. 2nd ed. London: Taylor & Hessey, 1818.

age he lived in: *Populo ut placerent.* I wish I had authority
to leave them out, but I have done all I could, set a mark
of reprobation upon them, throughout this edition." It is
strange that our fastidious critic should fall so soon from
praising to reprobating. The style of the familiar parts of
this comedy is indeed made up of conceits—low they may
be for what we know, but then they are not poor, but rich
ones. The scene of Launce with his dog (not that in the
second, but that in the fourth act) is a perfect treat in the
way of farcical drollery and invention; nor do we think
Speed's manner of proving his master to be in love defi-
cient in wit or sense, though the style may be criticized as
not simple enough for the modern taste.

Valentine. Why, how know you that I am in love?

Speed. Marry, by these special marks: first, you have learned,
  like Sir Protheus, to wreathe your arms like a malcontent,
  to relish a love song like a robin-red-breast, to walk alone like
  one that had the pestilence, to sigh like a schoolboy that had
  lost his A B C, to weep like a young wench that had buried
  her grandam, to fast like one that takes diet, to watch like
  one that fears robbing, to speak puling like a beggar at Hallowmas. You were wont, when you laughed, to crow like
  a cock; when you walked, to walk like one of the lions;
  when you fasted, it was presently after dinner; when you
  looked sadly, it was for want of money; and now you are
  metamorphosed with a mistress, that when I look on you,
  I can hardly think you my master.

The tender scenes in this play, though not so highly
wrought as in some others, have often much sweetness of
sentiment and expression. There is something pretty and
playful in the conversation of Julia with her maid, when
she shows such a disposition to coquetry about receiving
the letter from Proteus; and her behavior afterwards and
her disappointment, when she finds him faithless to his
vows, remind us at a distance of Imogen's tender constancy. Her answer to Lucetta, who advises her against
following her lover in disguise, is a beautiful piece of
poetry.

Lucetta. I do not seek to quench your love's hot fire,
　　But qualify the fire's extremest rage,
　　Lest it should burn above the bounds of reason.

Julia. The more thou damm'st it up, the more it burns;
　　The current that with gentle murmur glides,
　　Thou know'st, being stopp'd, impatiently doth rage;
　　But when his fair course is not hindered,
　　He makes sweet music with th' enamel'd stones,
　　Giving a gentle kiss to every sedge
　　He overtaketh in his pilgrimage:
　　And so by many winding nooks he strays,
　　With willing sport, to the wild ocean.
　　Then let me go, and hinder not my course;
　　I'll be as patient as a gentle stream,
　　And make a pastime of each weary step,
　　Till the last step have brought me to my love;
　　And there I'll rest, as after much turmoil,
　　A blessed soul doth in Elysium.

If Shakespear indeed had written only this and other passages in *The Two Gentlemen of Verona,* he would *almost* have deserved Milton's praise of him—

　　　　And sweetest Shakespeare, Fancy's child,
　　　　Warbles his native wood-notes wild.

But as it is, he deserves rather more praise than this.

GEORGE BERNARD SHAW

from *Our Theatres in the Nineties*

THE TWO GENTLEMEN OF VERONA. Daly's Theatre, 2 July
1895.   [6 *July* 1895]

The piece founded by Augustin Daly on Shakespear's
Two Gentlemen of Verona, to which I looked forward last
week, is not exactly a comic opera, though there is plenty
of music in it, and not exactly a serpentine dance, though
it proceeds under a play of changing colored lights. It is
something more old-fashioned than either: to wit, a vaudeville. And let me hasten to admit that it makes a very pleasant entertainment for those who know no better. Even I,
who know a great deal better, as I shall presently demon-
strate rather severely, enjoyed myself tolerably. I cannot
feel harshly towards a gentleman who works so hard as
Mr. Daly does to make Shakespear presentable: one feels
that he loves the bard, and lets him have his way as far
as he thinks it good for him. His rearrangement of the
scenes of the first two acts is just like him. Shakespear
shews lucidly how Proteus lives with his father (Antonio)
in Verona, and loves a lady of that city named Julia. Mr.
Daly, by taking the scene in Julia's house between Julia

From *Our Theatres in the Nineties* by George Bernard Shaw. 3 vols.
London: Constable & Co., Ltd., 1932. Reprinted by permission of the
Public Trustee and the Society of Authors.

and her maid, and the scene in Antonio's house between Antonio and Proteus, and making them into one scene, convinces the unlettered audience that Proteus and Julia live in the same house with their father Antonio. Further, Shakespear shews us how Valentine, the other gentleman of Verona, travels from Verona to Milan, the journey being driven into our heads by a comic scene in Verona, in which Valentine's servant is overwhelmed with grief at leaving his parents, and with indignation at the insensibility of his dog to his sorrow, followed presently by another comic scene in Milan in which the same servant is welcomed to the strange city by a fellow servant. Mr. Daly, however, is ready for Shakespeare on this point too. He just represents the two scenes as occurring in the same place; and immediately the puzzle as to who is who is complicated by a puzzle as to where is where. Thus is the immortal William adapted to the requirements of a nineteenth-century audience.

In preparing the text of his version Mr. Daly has proceeded on the usual principles, altering, transposing, omitting, improving, correcting, and transferring speeches from one character to another. Many of Shakespear's lines are mere poetry, not to the point, not getting the play along, evidently stuck in because the poet liked to spread himself in verse. On all such unbusinesslike superfluities Mr. Daly is down with his blue pencil. For instance, he relieves us of such stuff as the following, which merely conveys that Valentine loves Silvia, a fact already sufficiently established by the previous dialogue:

My thoughts do harbor with my Silvia nightly;
    And slaves they are to me, that send them flying:
Oh, could their master come and go as lightly,
    Himself would lodge where senseless they are lying.
My herald thoughts in thy pure bosom rest them,
    While I, their king, that thither them importune,
Do curse the grace that with such grace hath blessed them,
    Because myself do want my servant's fortune.
I curse myself, for they are sent by me,
    That they should harbor where their lord would be.

Slaves indeed are these lines and their like to Mr. Daly, who "sends them flying" without remorse. But when he comes to passages that a stage manager can understand, his reverence for the bard knows no bounds. The following awkward lines, unnecessary as they are under modern stage conditions, are at any rate not poetic, and are in the nature of police news. Therefore they are piously retained:

> What halloing, and what stir, is this today?
> These are my mates, that make their wills their law,
> Have some unhappy passenger in chase.
> They love me well; yet I have much to do,
> To keep them from uncivil outrages.
> Withdraw thee, Valentine: who's this comes here?

The perfunctory metrical character of such lines only makes them more ridiculous than they would be in prose. I would cut them out without remorse to make room for all the lines that have nothing to justify their existence except their poetry, their humor, their touches of character—in short, the lines for whose sake the play survives, just as it was for their sake it originally came into existence. Mr. Daly, who prefers the lines which only exist for the sake of the play, will doubtless think me as great a fool as Shakespear; but I submit to him, without disputing his judgment, that he is, after all, only a man with a theory of dramatic composition, going with a blue pencil over the work of a great dramatist, and striking out everything that does not fit his theory. Now, as it happens, nobody cares about Mr. Daly's theory; whilst everybody who pays to see what is, after all, advertised as a performance of Shakespear's play entitled *The Two Gentlemen of Verona,* and not as a demonstration of Mr. Daly's theory, does care more or less about the art of Shakespear. Why not give them what they ask for, instead of going to great trouble and expense to give them something else?

In those matters in which Mr. Daly has given the rein to his own taste and fancy: that is to say, in scenery, costumes, and music, he is for the most part disabled by a want of real knowledge of the arts concerned. I say for the most part, because his pretty fifteenth-century dresses, though probably inspired rather by Sir Frederic Leighton than by Benozzo Gozzoli, may pass. But the scenery is insufferable. First, for "a street in Verona" we get a Bath bun colored operatic front cloth with about as much light in it as there is in a studio in Fitzjohn's Avenue in the middle of October. I respectfully invite Mr. Daly to spend his next holiday looking at a real street in Verona, asking his conscience meanwhile whether a manager with eyes in his head and the electric light at his disposal could not advance a step on the Telbin (senior) style. Telbin was an admirable scene painter; but he was limited by the mechanical conditions of gas illumination; and he learnt his technique before the great advance made during the Impressionist movement in the painting of open-air effects, especially of brilliant sunlight. Of that advance Mr. Daly has apparently no conception. The days of Macready and Clarkson Stanfield still exist for him; he would probably prefer a water-color drawing of a foreign street by Samuel Prout to one of Mr. T. M. Rooke; and I daresay every relic of the original tallow candlelight that still clings to the art of scene painting is as dear to him as it is to most old playgoers, including, unhappily, many of the critics.

As to the elaborate set in which Julia makes her first entrance, a glance at it shews how far Mr. Daly prefers the Marble Arch to the loggia of Orcagna. All over the scene we have Renaissance work, in its genteelest stages of decay, held up as the perfection of romantic elegance and beauty. The school that produced the classicism of the First Empire, designed the terraces of Regent's Park and the façades of Fitzroy Square, and conceived the Boboli Gardens and Versailles as places for human beings to be happy in, ramps all over the scenery, and offers as much of its pet colonnades and statues as can be crammed into a single scene, by way of a compendium of everything that is lovely in the city of San Zeno and the tombs of the Scaligers. As to the natural objects depicted, I ask whether any man living has ever seen a pale green cypress in Verona or anywhere else out of a toy Noah's Ark. A man who, having once seen cypresses and felt their presence in a north Italian landscape, paints them lettuce color, must be suffering either from madness, malice, or a theory of how nature should have colored trees, cognate with Mr. Daly's theory of how Shakespear should have written plays.

Of the music let me speak compassionately. After all, it is only very lately that Mr. Arnold Dolmetsch, by playing fifteenth-century music on fifteenth-century instruments, has shewn us that the age of beauty was true to itself in music as in pictures and armor and costumes. But what should Mr. Daly know of this, educated as he no doubt was to believe that the court of Denmark should always enter in the first act of *Hamlet* to the march from *Judas Maccabaeus*? Schubert's setting of "Who Is Silvia?" he knew, but had rashly used up in *Twelfth Night* as "Who's Olivia." He has therefore had to fall back on another modern setting, almost supernaturally devoid of any particular merit. Besides this, all through the drama the most horribly common music repeatedly breaks out on the slightest pretext or on no pretext at all. One dance, set to a crude old English popular tune, sundry eighteenth and nineteenth century musical banalities, and a titivated plantation melody in the first act which produces an indescribably atrocious effect by coming in behind the scenes as a sort of coda to Julia's curtain speech, all turn the play, as I have said, into a vaudeville. Needless to add, the accompaniments are not played on lutes and viols, but by the orchestra and a guitar or two. In the forest scene the outlaws begin the act by a chorus. After their encounter with Valentine they go off the stage singing the refrain exactly in the style of *La Fille de Madame Angot*. The wanton absurdity of introducing this comic opera convention is presently eclipsed by a thunderstorm, immediately after which Valentine enters and delivers his speech sitting down on a bank of moss, as an outlaw in tights naturally would after a terrific shower. Such is the effect of many years of theatrical management on the human brain.

Perhaps the oddest remark I have to make about the performance is that, with all its glaring defects and blunders, it is rather a handsome and elaborate one as such things go. It is many years now since Mr. Ruskin first took the Academicians of his day aback by the obvious remark that Carpaccio and Giovanni Bellini were better painters than Domenichino and Salvator Rosa. Nobody dreams now of assuming that Pope was a greater poet than Chaucer, that Mozart's Twelfth Mass is superior to the masterpieces of Orlandus Lassus and Palestrina, or that our "ecclesiastical Gothic" architecture is more enlightened than Norman axe work. But the theatre is still wallowing in such follies; and until Mr. Comyns Carr and Sir Edward Burne-Jones, Baronet, put King Arthur on the stage more or less in the manner natural to men who know these things, Mr. Daly might have pleaded the unbroken conservatism of the playhouse against me. But after the Lyceum scenery and architecture I decline to accept a relapse without protest. There is no reason why cheap photographs of Italian architecture (sixpence apiece in infinite variety at the bookstall in the South Kensington Museum) should not rescue us from Regent's Park Renaissance colonnades on the stage just as the electric light can rescue us from Telbin's dun-colored sunlight. The opera is the last place in the world where any wise man would look for adequate stage illusion; but the fact is that Mr. Daly, with all his colored lights, has not produced a single Italian scene comparable in illusion to that provided by Sir Augustus Harris at Covent Garden for *Cavalleria Rusticana.*

Of the acting I have not much to say. Miss Rehan provided a strong argument in favor of rational dress by looking much better in her page's costume than in that of her own sex; and in the serenade scene, and that of the wooing of Silvia for Proteus, she stirred some feeling into the part, and reminded us of what she was in *Twelfth Night,* where the same situations are fully worked out. For the rest, she moved and spoke with imposing rhythmic grace. That is as much notice as so cheap a part as Julia is worth from an artist who, being absolute mistress of the situation at Daly's Theatre, might and should have played Imogen for us instead. The two gentlemen were impersonated by Mr. Worthing and Mr. Craig. Mr. Worthing charged himself with feeling without any particular reference to his lines; and Mr. Craig struck a balance by attending to the meaning of his speeches without taking them at all to heart. Mr. Clarke, as the Duke, was emphatic, and worked up every long speech to a climax in the useful old style; but his tone is harsh, his touch on his consonants coarse, and his accent ugly, all fatal disqualifications for the delivery of Shakespearean verse. The scenes between Launce and his dog brought out the latent silliness and childishness of the audience as Shakespear's clowning scenes always do: I laugh at them like a yokel myself. Mr. Lewis hardly made the most of them. His style has been formed in modern comedies, where the locutions are so familiar that their meaning is in no danger of being lost by the rapidity of his quaint utterance; but Launce's phraseology is another matter: a few of the funniest lines missed fire because the audience did not catch them. And with all possible allowance for Mr. Daly's blue pencil, I cannot help suspecting that Mr. Lewis's memory was responsible for one or two of his omissions. Still, Mr. Lewis has always his comic force, whether he makes the most or the least of it; so that he cannot fail in such a part as Launce. Miss Maxine Elliot's Silvia was the most considerable performance after Miss Rehan's Julia. The whole company will gain by the substitution on Tuesday next of a much better play, *A Midsummer Night's Dream,* as a basis for Mr. Daly's operations. No doubt he is at this moment, like Mrs. Todgers, "a dodgin' among the tender bits with a fork, and an eatin' of 'em"; but there is sure to be enough of the original left here and there to repay a visit.

H. B. CHARLTON

from *Shakespearian Comedy*

In its first intention, Elizabethan romantic comedy was an attempt to adapt the world of romance and all its implications to the service of comedy. *The Two Gentlemen of Verona* shows that intention at its crudest. In the story of it, there are all the main marks of the medieval tradition as that tradition had been modified, elaborated, and extended by the idealism of Petrarch and by the speculations of the Platonists. It is yet the same tradition in its essence, corroborated rather than altered by the modifying factors; as, for instance, at the hands of Ficino, Platonism brought a medico-metaphysical theory to explain the love-laden gleam of a beautiful eye. Shakespeare's play embodies a literary manner and a moral code; its actions are conducted according to a conventional etiquette and are determined by a particular creed; and every feature of it, in matter and in sentiment, is traceable to the romantic attitude of man to woman. It presents as its setting a world constituted in such fashion that the obligations and the sanctions of its doctrines could best be realized. The course of the whole play is determined by the values such doctrine attaches to the love of man and woman.

A note struck early in the play recalls one of the few passionate love stories of classical legend—"how young

From *Shakespearian Comedy* by H. B. Charlton. London: Methuen and Co., Ltd.; New York: The Macmillan Company. 1938. Reprinted by permission of Methuen and Co., Ltd.

Leander crossed the Hellespont"—and at another moment, Ariadne is remembered "passioning for Theseus' perjury." But the real color of the tale is given unmistakably by the presence amongst its characters of Sir Eglamour. By his name is he known and whence he springs. He points straight back to the source of the religious cult of love: "servant and friend" of Sylvia, he is ready at call to rush to any service to which she may command him. His own lady and his true love died, and on her grave he vowed pure chastity, dedicating himself to the assistance of lovers in affliction, recking nothing what danger should betide him in the venture. His home is in the land of medieval romance; and his brethren are those consecrated warriors who will undertake all danger, though it stands next to death, for one calm look of Love's approval. He comes to life again in a play where knightly vows are spoken, where errantry is the normal mode of service, where the exercise of tilt and tournament is the traditional recreation, where lovers name themselves habitually the servants of their ladies, where such service may impose as a duty the helping of one's lady to a rival, and where the terms of infamy to which the utmost slander can give voice are "perjured, false, disloyal." And that is the world in which Shakespeare makes his Two Gentlemen live.

Throughout the play, "Love's a mighty lord,"

> There is no woe to his correction
> Nor to his service no such joy on earth.

This is the state of the lover as the old *Romaunt of the Rose* had depicted it:

> The sore of love is merveilous,
> For now is the lover joyous,
> Now can he pleyne, now can he grone,
> Now can he syngen, now maken mone;
> To day he pleyneth for hevynesse,
> To morowe he pleyeth for jolynesse.
> The lyf of love is full contrarie,
> Which stounde-mele can ofte varie.

Heavy penance is visited on unbelievers

for contemning Love,
Whose high imperious thoughts will punish him
With bitter fasts, with penitential groans,
With nightly tears and daily heartsore sighs.

Sleep is chased from such a rebel's now enthralled eyes,
to make them watchers of his own heart's sorrow. From
true votaries, nothing less than absolute devotion is required. They must hold no discourse except it be of love.
Absent from their lady, they must let no single hour o'erslip
without its ceremonial sigh for her sake. The more such
languishing fidelity appears to be spurned, the more must
it grow and fawn upon its recalcitrant object. Apart from
love, nothing in life has the least significance:

banished from her,
Is self from self, a deadly banishment.
What light is light, if Sylvia be not seen?
What joy is joy, if Sylvia be not by?
Except I be by Sylvia in the night,
There is no music in the nightingale.
Unless I look on Sylvia in the day,
There is no day for me to look upon.
She is my essence, and I leave to be,
If I am not by her fair influence
Fostered, illumined, cherished, kept alive.

Such is the consecrated desolation of the romantic lover:
the medieval sense of a world emptied of its content per-
sists through romantic poetry and is the undertone of the
Renaissance sonneteers' woe. Bembo puts it not unlike
Valentine in the play:

Tu m'hai lasciato senza sole i giorni,
Le notte senza stelle, e grave e egro
Tutto questo, ond'io parlo, ond'io respiro:
La terra scossa, e'l ciel turbato e negro;
Et pien di mille oltraggi e mille scorni
Me sembra ogni parte, quant'io miro.

> Valor e cortesia si dipartiro
> Nel tuo partire, e'l mondo infermo giacque;
> Et virtu spense i suoi chiari lumi;
> Et le fontane e i fiumi
> Nega la vena antica e l'usate acque:
> Et gli augelletti abandonaro il canto,
> Et l'herbe e i fior lasciar nude le piaggie,
> Ne piu di fronde il bosco si conesperse.

But the lover has ample recompense for his sorrow. Setting the world at nought, he gains a heaven in its stead:

> she is mine own,
> And I as rich in having such a jewel
> As twenty seas if all their sand were pearl,
> The water nectar, and the rocks pure gold.

Inevitably, a creed of such ardent devotion has its appropriate liturgy. Stuffed with protestation, and full of new-found oaths, the lover utters his fears in wailful sonnets, whose composed rhymes are fully fraught with serviceable vows:

> . . . and on the altar of her beauty
> You sacrifice your tears, your sighs, your heart:
> Write till your ink be dry, and with your tears
> Moist it again, and frame some feeling line
> That may discover such integrity:
> For Orpheus' lute was strung with poets' sinews,
> Whose golden touch could soften steel and stones,
> Make tigers tame, and huge leviathans
> Forsake unsounded deeps to dance on sands.
> After your dire-lamenting elegies,
> Visit by night your lady's chamber window
> With some sweet concert; to their instruments
> Tune a deploring dump: the night's dead silence
> Will well become such sweet-complaining grievance.
> This, or else nothing, will inherit her.

With oceans of tears, and twenty thousand soul-confirming oaths, the lover excites himself to a fervid bacchanalian orgy, and in his braggardism proclaims his lady "sovereign

to all the creatures on the earth," threatening destruction
to all who will not at once subscribe, and extermination to
any who but dare to breathe upon her. In the intervals of
these ecstatic outbursts, the lover stands before the picture
of his love, sighing and weeping, wreathing his arms like
a malcontent, until at length he walks off alone like one
that hath the pestilence.

When cruel circumstance separates him from his lady,
etiquette prescribes the proper behavior and the right de-
meanor. He resorts to the congenial solitude of woods or
wilderness. In the earlier days of the cult, his manner on
these occasions was more violent than ceremonious. Tris-
tan, as Malory tells us, exiled and separated from his love,
goes mad for grief; he would unlace his armor and go into
the wilderness, where he "brast down the trees and bowes,
and otherwhyle, when he found the harp that the lady sent
him, then wold he harpe and playe therupon and wepe
togethre." But in the course of time the manners of soli-
taries became more polite. Chaucer (or the author of the
Romaunt of the Rose) advises the lover to cultivate a
proper solitude:

> For ofte, whan thou bithenkist thee
> Of thy lovyng, where so thou be,
> Fro folk thou must departe in hie,
> That noon perceyve thi maladie.
> But hyde thyne harme thou must alone,
> And go forthe sole, and make thy mone.

It is only one more stage to the final artistic decorum of
the habit. The lover in the French romance *Flamenca* "in
the dark of night goes of custom to listen to the nightingale
in the wood." Just, in fact, as does Valentine: in the intervals between inspecting the arms or allocating the booty
of his bandit band, he takes his laments for Sylvia into the
woods for orchestral effects from the nightingales:

> These shadowy, desert, unfrequented woods
> I better brook than flourishing peopled towns:
> Here can I sit alone, unseen of any,

And to the nightingale's complaining notes
Tune my distresses and record my woes.

Such is the way of lovers in romances, and in *The Two
Gentlemen of Verona*. Their state of spiritual ecstasy is
revealed by the progressive etherialization of their sus-
tenance. A collection of the menus of romantic feasts is
more than a gastronomic document. In the beginnings of
romance, eating and drinking was a major occupation.
Owein ate and drank "whilst it was late in the time of the
nones"; and once he was bidden to a feast which took
three months to consume and had taken three years to
prepare. But later, the initiate have so far purged their
mortal grossness that eating and loving begin to appear
incompatible. Again the *Romaunt of the Rose* brings the
evidence:

> Such comyng and such goyng
> Such hevynesse and such wakyng
> Makith lovers, withouten wene,
> Under her clothes pale and lene.
> For love leveth colour ne cleernesse,
> Who loveth trewe hath no fatnesse;
> Thou shalt wel by thy-silf ysee
> That thou must nedis assaied be;
> For men that shape hem other weye
> Falsly her ladyes to bitraye,
> It is no wonder though they be fatt,
> With false othes her loves they gatt.
> For oft I see suche losengours
> Fatter than abbatis or priours.

On occasion, the true lover, like Jehan in *Jehan and
Blonde,* is like to fade away, and can only eat when his
lady serves the dishes to him with her own delicate hands.
Our Valentine had been a good trencherman before he
became a romantic lover; in those days, when he fasted,
it was presently after dinner. But once he becomes a votary, not even ambrosia nor nectar is good enough for his
ethereal table: "now can I break my fast, dine, sup, and
sleep upon the very naked name of love." How he thrives

on this diet will become a primary article of the literary and dramatic criticism of *The Two Gentlemen of Verona*.

So much for the spirit of romance in the play. Now for the world in which it is set—since, taking its religion thence, it must also take the romantic world in which such religion may reveal itself. Not men living dully sluggardized at home, but those bred and tutored in the wider world, seeking preferment out, trying their fortunes in war or discovering islands far away—these are they who have scope to put such religion to the proof. So in *The Two Gentlemen of Verona,* the scene is laid in Italy, the country which to Shakespeare's fellows was the hallowed land of romance. But it is an Italy of romance, not of physiographic authenticity. It has inland waterways unknown to geographers; the journey from Verona to Mantua is a sea voyage; it is indeed a scenario in which all the material trappings of romance may be assembled. Mountain and forest are indispensable, mountains which are brigand-haunted, and forests in the gloom of which are abbeys from whose postern gates friars creep into the encircling woods, so wrapt in penitential mood that lurking lions, prowling hungrily for food, are utterly forgotten. In such a locality, the tale of true love may run its uneven course. The poetically gifted lover meets such obstacles as a rival, at whom he hurls his cartel, and a perverse father whose plans for his daughter are based on such irrelevant considerations as the rivals' bank balances. The father's castle has its upper tower far from the ground, and built so shelving that to climb it is at apparent hazard of one's life. And here is the angelic daughter's chamber wherein she is nightly lodged, within doors securely locked, so that rescue can only be by a corded ladder to her chamber window. Then unexpected difficulties will be expected to intrude: the best-laid plot to carry her away is foiled by the machinations of a villain out of the least suspected quarter. Banishment naturally follows, and at length, with the flight of the heroine and the pursuit of her by the entire court, all will work out well by a series of surprising coincidences, to which rivals, brigands, friars, and lions are all somehow contributory. In this way, romantic love makes its romantic universe; and this in fact is the setting and the story of *The Two Gentlemen of Verona.*

This, both in matter and in spirit, is the tradition which the Elizabethan dramatists desired to lift bodily onto their comic stage. But something somehow went wrong. The spirit of medieval romance seemed to shrivel in the presence of comedy. Something similar had in fact happened in the real world outside the theater. The last hero of romance had lived gloriously and had died quite out of his part. Jacques de Lalaing, le bon chevalier, the mirror of knighthood who adorned the Burgundian court in the middle of the fifteenth century, had become the pattern of chivalry for all Europe. To his contemporaries, "fair was he as Paris, pious as Aeneas, wise as Ulysses, and passionate as Hector": and his exploits in tournament and in knight-errantry had carried his fame through many lands. He died an early death in 1453. But he did not die of a lover's broken heart; nor was he slain in tourney by a foeman worthy of his steel and of his thirty-two emblazoned pennants. He was shot down by a cannon ball in an expedition against the merchants and shopkeepers of Ghent. The gross ponderable facts of a very material world swept the symbol of an outworn ideal from off the face of the earth. So in *The Two Gentlemen,* a sheer clod of earth, Launce by name, will, quite unwittingly, expose the unsubstantiality of the romantic hero with whom the play throws him into contact. But we are anticipating. The consequences of Shakespeare's attempt to dramatize romance must be watched in closer detail.

There is little wonder that the Elizabethan dramatists saw the dramatic possibilities of such material, and did not at first perceive its dramatic disadvantages. They felt the dramatic thrill of following these lovers and setting the world at nought. Nor is it very difficult to set the geographical world at nought, at least to the extent of making inland seas in Italy or liberating living lions in its woods. Yet sometimes the distortions of the physical universe necessarily ventured by the romanticist entail violent wrenches of our common consciousness. The dukes of Shakespeare's Italy, for instance, apparently have magic power over the flight of time; for whilst a banished man is speaking but ten lines, the proclamation of his banishment is ratified, promulgated, and has become publicly known throughout the duchy, and sentinels have already been posted along the frontiers to prevent a surreptitious return of the exile to the land which he has not yet had time to pack his suitcase for leaving. It is a land too where optical illusions, or perhaps optical delusions, are the normal way of vision. A man seeking a page boy interviews an applicant for the post; he is just enough of a businessman to know that some sort of reason must be advanced for taking on a servant who can show neither character nor reference from previous employers, and so Proteus, engaging the disguised Julia, says that the engagement is specifically on the recommendation of the applicant's face; but he does not recognize, as he gazes into this face, that it was the one he was smothering with kisses a few weeks before when its owner, in her proper dress, was his betrothed. Yet these are really only minor impediments, requiring but a little and a by no means reluctant suspension of our disbelief. They are altogether insignificant compared with the reservations involved when romance displays its peculiar propensity for setting the world of man at nought. To satisfy its own obligations, it perforce demanded supermen; at all events, the heroes it puts forward as its votaries in the play are something either more or less than men.

Romantically speaking, Valentine is the hero, and not alone in the technical sense. In classical comedy the hero is simply the protagonist, the central figure who is the biggest butt of the comic satire. But here the protagonist is the upholder of the faith on which the play is built, the man with whom the audience is called upon to rejoice admiringly, and not the fellow at whom it is derisively to laugh. He is to play the hero in every sense of the word. Yet in the event, the prevailing spirit of romance endows him with sentiments and provides him with occupations which inevitably frustrate the heroic intention. The story renders him a fool. Convention may sanctify his sudden conversion from the mocker to the votary of love, and may even excuse or palliate his fractious braggardism when he insults Proteus with ill-mannered comparisons between Silvia and Julia. But his helplessness and his impenetrable stupidity amount to more than the traditional blindness of a lover. Even the clown Speed can see through Silvia's trick, when she makes Valentine write a letter to himself. But Valentine plays out the excellent motion as an exceeding puppet, unenlightened by the faintest gleam of common insight. And despite his vaunt that he knows Proteus as well as he knows himself, he is blind to villainies so palpable that Launce, the other clown of the piece, though he be but a fool, has the wits to recognize them for what they plainly are. The incidents are dramatically very significant, for both Launce and Speed come into the play for no reason whatever but to be unmistakable dolts. One begins to feel that it will be extremely difficult to make a hero of a man who is proved to be duller of wit than the patent idiots of the piece. Even when Valentine might have shone by resource in action, he relapses into conventional laments, and throws himself helplessly into the arms of Proteus for advice and consolation. Heroic opportunity stands begging round him when he encounters the brigands. But besides demonstrating that he can tell a lie— witness his tale of cock and bull about having killed a man —the situation only serves to discredit him still more: for the words of his lie, his crocodile tears for the fictitious man he claims to have slain, and his groundless boast that he slew him manfully in fight without false vantage or base treachery, are in fact nothing but an attempt to make moral capital by means of forgery and perjury. They have not even the recommendation of the Major General's tears for the orphan boy. When at length Valentine is duly installed as captain of the brigands, his chief occupation is to vary highway robbery with sentimental descants on the beauty of nature in her "shadowy, desert, unfrequented woods":

Here can I sit alone, unseen of any—

and we already know his favorite hobby on these saunterings—

And to the nightingale's complaining notes
Tune my distresses and record my woes.

He is own brother to Gilbert's coster, who, when he isn't jumping on his mother, loves to lie abasking in the sun, and to the cutthroat, who, when not occupied in crimes, loves to hear the little brook agurgling and listen to the merry village chimes. But Valentine's utmost reach of ineptitude comes with what, again romantically speaking, is meant to be the heroic climax of the play. When he has just learnt the full tale of the villainy of Proteus, the code permits him neither resentment nor passion. Like a cashier addressing a charwoman who has pilfered a penny stamp, he sums up his rebuke——"I am sorry I must never trust thee more." And worse follows immediately. With but five lines of formal apology from the villain, Valentine professes himself so completely satisfied that he enthusiastically resigns his darling Silvia to the traitor. Even Valentine must have seen that the gesture was a little odd, because he quotes the legal sanction. It is the code, a primary article in the romantic faith——"that my love may appear plain and free." But it makes a man a nincompoop. Nor does it help much that after this preposterous episode Valentine is allowed to spit a little fire in an encounter with another rival, Thurio. He has already proved himself so true a son of romance that he can never again be mistaken for a creature of human nature.

Proteus is less hampered by romantic obligations; because the plot requires him to have just sufficient of salutary villainy to make him throw over their commandments for his own ends. Yet the villain of romance suffers almost as much from the pressure of romanticism as does the hero. The noble fellows whom he, as villain, is called upon to deceive are such gullible mortals that little positive skill is necessary. Proteus can fool Thurio and Valentine and the Duke without exerting himself. But on the one occasion when he might have shown his wits, he only reveals his lack of them. Making love to Silvia, he meets her protest against his disloyalty to Julia by inventing the easy excuse that Julia is dead. Silvia replies that, even so, he should be ashamed to wrong Valentine. It is, of course, a tight corner: but the best Proteus can do is to say "I likewise hear that Valentine is dead." He might at least have displayed a little more ingenuity in invention; he fails in precisely such a situation as would have permitted the clown of classical comedy to triumph. Moreover, the main plot requires Proteus to be guilty of incredible duplicity, and of the most facile rapidity in changing morals and mistresses. But he need scarcely have made the change explicit in words so ineptly casual and banal as his remark: *"Methinks* my zeal to Valentine is cold." The phrase is accidentally in keeping with the unintended complacence he displays when, wooing the lady who will have none of him, he begins by informing her that "he has made her happy" by his coming. The trait becomes intolerably ludicrous when, all his sins forgiven him, and Julia restored to his arms, all he can utter in confession is his own fatuous self-conceit:

> O heaven, were man
> But constant, he were perfect.

It is, of course, a fine sentiment; but the audience, having seen Valentine, simply will not believe it.

Even the brigands of romance will scarcely stand the test of the stage. They enter with metaphorical daggers in mouths bristling with black mustachios and with desperate oaths. Callous and bloodthirsty ruffians, spoiling for a fight, their chief regret is that fate is sending only one defenseless traveler to be rifled instead of ten. But when the destined victim turns out to be two, courage perhaps abates a little: at all events, the travelers are warned to keep their distance, and throw over the booty or otherwise to assume a sitting posture, whilst the rifling is safely done by the desperadoes themselves. Perhaps this, and not his customary ineptitude in speech, is what makes Valentine address the villains as "My friends." But, of course, his assumption is, for the trade of brigandage, economically unsound. And so, with apologies for correcting him, Valentine is informed that he is not playing the game—"that's not so,

sir; we are your enemies." But the outlaws are connois-
seurs of masculine beauty, and Valentine's fine figure se-
cures him an opportunity for a hearing: one cannot but
note that this is the first time that any of his romantic at-
tributes has made for his advantage, and that he misuses
it scandalously for his lying brag. Hearing the fiction, however, the bandits feel at once that here is a fellow spirit,
given, like themselves, to "so small a fault" as homicide.
Straightway they implore him to show them his diploma
in the modern languages, promising him the kingship of
the band if it is of good honors' standard. Becoming con-
vivial, they reveal their amiable dispositions in snatches
of their life history. One has amused himself with attempts
at abduction. Another, when the whim takes him, "in his
mood," has the merry trick of stabbing gentlemen unto the
heart; and his gaiety makes us forget that a mood in Shakespeare's English was not quite the casual fancy it now is.
Another acclaims these and other "such like petty crimes"
as congenial peccadilloes in his own repertory. By this
time, the brigands have become so hilarious with their
reminiscences, that they are no longer minded to scrutinize
Valentine's academic credentials. They will take him for
a linguist merely "on his own report," and, mainly because
he "is beautified with goodly shape," they offer him the
leadership, pathetically promising to love him as their commander and their king. Clearly such a thoroughly unbrig-
andlike procedure as this election has almost put them out
of their parts. They must be allowed to recover in a traditional tableau. Daggers are whipped out, threats become
fierce, and Valentine, with steel points at his throat, is
given the choice of being a king or a corpse. Perhaps his
fear is responsible for the odd proviso that "silly women"
shall be exempt from the depredations of the gang over
which he is to rule; but it is of course too much to expect
of better men than Valentine to require them to anticipate
a variation in the meaning of a word. Neither before nor
after *The Two Gentlemen of Verona* has dramatic literature known a band of outlaws like to these—except once:
there are the Pirates of Penzance: but then Gilbert meant
his to be funny.

One begins to suspect that everything which is hallowed by the tradition of romance is made thereby of no avail for the purposes of drama. But there are Julia and Launce to reckon with; and these are figures universally accounted the most substantial beings in the play. So indeed they are. But they owe it entirely to the fact that they are under no obligation whatever to the code of romance. The behavior of Valentine is entirely conditioned by the doctrine of romantic love. But the code allowed to woman no duty but to excite by her beauty the devoted worship of her knight. If England instead of France had performed the final codification of chivalry, its women might have had other and less ladylike propensities, such, for instance, as King Horn's Rimenhild displayed. But when a French romance elaborates its portrait of womanhood, it gives her patience rather than character: women with the forcefulness of a distinct personality might have turned the energies of their knights away from consecrated paths of knighthood, as Chretien's Enide turned her Erec:

> Mes tant l'ama Erec d'amors
> Que d'armes mes ne li chaloit,
> Ne a tornoiemant n'aloit
> N'avoit mes soing de tornoiier.

Wherefore Chretien's romance tells of Erec's regeneration through the discipline by which he reduces his Enide to absolute submission. At the end, she has attained complete self-suppression—

> Ne je tant hardie ne sui
> Que je os regarder vers lui—

and, to the modern eye, has become the perfect pattern of an exquisitely charming nonentity.

When Shakespeare takes over a tradition whose women are like these, so long as he preserves the beauty of their faces, he can endow them with whatever character he may please. His Julia is a creation, not a convention. As she is a woman, acting on a woman's instinct—"I have no other but a woman's reason, I think him so because I think him so"—she is depicted in moods, whimsies, and vagaries which are in fact the stuff of dramatic characterization. Like the heroine of romance, she will cover her first love letter with kisses and press the precious manuscript to her heart. But like the spirited independent young lady of the world, she will not expose herself to the chuckles of her maid by exhibiting the common symptoms of her affections. Hence the pretended contempt, and the struggle to keep up appearances, even at considerable risk to the sacred document. But for what seriously concerns her love, Julia is too levelheaded to overreach herself. As far as may be, she will avoid the disapproval of opinion: but where there is no remedy, she will defy a scandalized world and undertake her pilgrimage of love. She knows the hazards of the road and the many weary steps it will involve. But she also knows her own capacities, and has duly taken note of all material things she will stand in need of. And although Proteus is a poor thing on whom to lavish so much love, Julia knows that love is indeed a blinded god; and in her capable hands even a Proteus may be molded to something worth the having.

Launce is another who insists on remaining in the memory. He has no real right within the play, except that gentlemen must have servants and Elizabethan audiences must have clowns. But coming in thus by a back door, he earns an unexpected importance in the play. Seen side by side with Speed, his origin is clear. Whilst Speed belongs to the purely theatrical family of the Dromios, with their punning and logic-chopping asininities, Launce harks back to the native Costard. And as Costard shows his relationship to Bottom by his skill in village theatricals, so Launce reveals by his wooing his family connection with Touchstone, and Touchstone's Audrey, who was a poor thing, but his own. All the kind of the Launces are thus palpably a mighty stock. Their worth, compared with that of the Speeds and the Dromios, is admirably indicated by Launce's consummate use of Speed's curiosity and of his better schooling. Launce gets his letter deciphered; he gets also an opportunity to display his own superior breeding and to secure condign punishment for the ill-mannered Speed: "now will he be swinged for reading my letter; an unmannerly slave, that will thrust himself into secrets! I'll after, to rejoice in the boy's correction."

Launce is happiest with his dog. Clownage can go no farther than the pantomimic representation, with staff and shoe and dog, of the parting from his home folks. Laughter is hilarious at Launce's bitter grief that his ungrateful cur declined to shed a tear. That Launce should expect it is, of course, the element of preposterous incongruity which makes him a clown. But when he puts his complaint squarely, that his "dog has no more pity in him than a dog," the thrust pierces more than it was meant to. Romance itself has expected no less largely of Valentine, of Proteus, and of the rest. It has demanded that man shall be more than man, and has laid upon him requisitions passing the ability of man to fulfill. At the bidding of romance, Valentine and Proteus have become what they are in the play, and the one thing they are not is men like other men. A further incident in which Launce is concerned takes on a similarly unexpected significance. He has made as great a sacrifice as did Valentine himself: he has given up his own cur in place of the one which Proteus entrusted to him to take to Silvia. But the effect hardly suggests that self-sacrifice is worldly-wise. And so once more it seems to bring into question the worldly worth of the code which sanctifies such deeds. Unintentionally, Launce has become the means by which the incompatibilities and the unrealities of romantic postulates are laid bare. And Launce is palpably the stuff of comedy: awakening our comedy sense, he inevitably sharpens our appreciation of the particular range of incongruities which are the province of comedy—the incongruity between what a thing really is and what it is taken to be.

Romance, and not comedy, has called the tune of *The Two Gentlemen of Verona* and governed the direction of the action of the play. That is why its creatures bear so little resemblance to men of flesh and blood. Lacking this, they are scarcely dramatic figures at all; for every form of drama would appear to seek at least so much of human nature in its characters. But perhaps the characters of the Two Gentlemen are comic in a sense which at first had never entered the mind of their maker. Valentine bids for the sympathy, but not for the laughter of the audience: the ideals by which he lives are assumed to have the world's approbation. But in execution they involve him in most ridiculous plight. He turns the world from its compassionate approval to a mood of skeptical questioning. The hero of romantic comedy appears no better than its clowns. And so topsy-turvy is the world of romance that apparently the one obvious way to be reputed in it for a fool is to show at least a faint sign of discretion and of common sense. Thurio, for instance, was cast for the dotard of the play, and of course he is not without egregious folly. But what was meant in the end to annihilate him with contempt turns out quite otherwise. Threatened by Valentine's sword, he resigns all claim to Silvia, on the ground that he holds him but a fool that will endanger his body for a girl that loves him not. The audience is invited to call Thurio a fool for thus showing himself to be the one person in the play with a modicum of worldly wisdom, a respect for the limitations of human nature, and a recognition of the conditions under which it may survive. Clearly, Shakespeare's first attempt to make romantic comedy had only succeeded so far that it had unexpectedly and inadvertently made romance comic. The real problem was still to be faced.

MARK VAN DOREN

from *Shakespeare*

In its kind *The Two Gentlemen of Verona* is not nearly as good as *The Taming of the Shrew* is in the kind called farce. But Shakespeare will soon do better in the kind he now discovers, and with one exception, *The Merry Wives of Windsor,* he is never to follow any other. *The Two Gentlemen of Verona* is a slight comedy and it minces uncertainly to an implausible conclusion, but it is Shakespeare's own and it sets his course. His problem henceforth is not to keep his fun outside the range of feeling but to keep his feeling within the range of fun; or rather it is to mingle them so that wit and emotion are wedded in an atmosphere which is as grave as it is smiling, as golden as it is bright. This atmosphere, so natural to man's life, so easy to breathe, and so mellow in its hue, is uniquely Shakespeare's, and it will be sufficient for his purposes in comedy; in its amber light he can go anywhere and consider everything, and his people can speak with the richest variety. Its elements are scarcely compounded in *The Two Gentlemen of Verona,* which is only a copy of what is to come; but for that very reason they are separately recognizable, they can be witnessed in the process of creation.

Valentine's opening speech announces the tone as he discourses to his fellow gentleman concerning the advan-

From *Shakespeare* by Mark Van Doren. New York: Henry Holt and Co., 1939; London: George Allen & Unwin, Ltd., 1941. Copyright 1939 by Mark Van Doren. Reprinted by permission of Holt, Rinehart and Winston, Inc.

tages of travel. "Such wind as scatters young men through the world" will soon blow both the heroes—rather stiff and humorless figures, newborn in Shakespeare's comic universe—from Verona to Milan, where one of them will forget his beloved Julia and plot to steal the other's Silvia. So far they are at peace, and their voices move lightly through the cadences of a graceful, breeze-haunted music. Valentine's speech is indeed a poem:

> Cease to persuade, my loving Proteus.
> Home-keeping youth have ever homely wits.
> Were 't not affection chains thy tender days
> To the sweet glances of thy honor'd love,
> I rather would entreat thy company
> To see the wonders of the world abroad
> Than, living dully sluggardiz'd at home,
> Wear out thy youth with shapeless idleness.
> But since thou lov'st, love still and thrive therein,
> Even as I would when I to love begin.
>
> (I.i.1–10)

The rhyme at the end is amateur, but Valentine has caught the tone which will be heard henceforth in the golden world of gentlemen where Shakespeare's comedy will occur. It is a world whose free and graceful movement finds a symbol for itself in the travel of young men:

> Some to the wars, to try their fortune there;
> Some to discover islands far away;
> Some to the studious universities.
>
> (I.iii.8–10)

They are awaited somewhere by ladies of fine and disciplined feeling; or they will be followed, as Proteus in the present case is followed by Julia, in brave disguise and be served as pages by the very sweethearts they have lost. The ladies will be accustomed to compliment:

Valentine.   Sweet lady, entertain him
To be my fellow servant to your ladyship. . . .

Silvia. Servant, you are welcome to a worthless mistress.

Proteus. I'll die on him that says so but yourself.

Silvia. That you are welcome?

Proteus.   That you are worthless.
                                         (II.iv.103–04, 112–14)

In their grace they understand the arts both of bestowing and of receiving praise. And their ideal might be such a man as Eglamour, whom Silvia invites to be her escort as she follows Valentine:

> Thyself hast lov'd; and I have heard thee say
> No grief did ever come so near thy heart
> As when thy lady and thy true love died. . . .
> I do desire thee, even from a heart
> As full of sorrows as the sea of sands,
> To bear me company.

                                         (IV.iii.19–21, 33–35)

They are not wailing women; their grief is delicate, well-taught, tender, and half-concealed. They are at home in romance: Valentine must climb to Silvia by a corded ladder, Julia must knit up her hair in silken strings with twenty odd-conceited truelove knots (II.vii. 45–46), and there will be outlaws in the dangerous forest—hardly dangerous themselves, once a sweet lady adventures among them. And they live for that love which is both "a mighty lord" (II.iv. 135) and as tenderly capricious as

> The uncertain glory of an April day   (I.iii.85)

So do their gentlemen live for love of each other. Friendship is one of the gods here, and he has given laws which Proteus will find it going against the grain to break, so that soliloquies will be necessary before he can comprehend the depth of his default. He has not heard Valentine describe him to the Duke of Milan, but the language would have been familiar:

I knew him as myself, for from our infancy
We have convers'd and spent our hours together;
And though myself have been an idle truant,
Omitting the sweet benefit of time
To clothe mine age with angel-like perfection,
Yet hath Sir Proteus, for that's his name,
Made use and fair advantage of his days. . . .
He is complete in feature and in mind
With all good grace to grace a gentleman.

                              (II.iv.61–67, 72–73)

It is such a friend that Proteus betrays, and his exclamation at the close, after the reconciliation which no one believes,

                    O heaven! Were man
        But constant, he were perfect. That one error
        Fills him with faults,

                              (V.iv.110–12)

covers his untruth to Valentine no less than his abandonment of Julia.

"Heaven-bred poesy," as the Duke puts it, is natural to the mood of this world. And music is so much so that we cannot be surprised to find an excellent sweet song, Who is Silvia, built into the key scene of the play—laced firmly into it with more than simple irony, for Julia, who hears it sung to her rival, does not know that Proteus is pretending to sing it for Thurio. Nor can we fail to note the balances set up here and there—between Julia's coyness (I.ii) and Silvia's (II.i), between Proteus's concealment of a letter (I.iii) and Valentine's concealment of a ladder (III.i)—as phrases are balanced in music. And the favorite subjects for quibble are note, burden, sharp, flat, bass, string, and change.

Of quibbles there are many in the play; too many, since they are the only device yet known by Shakespeare for securing the effect of wit and he must overwork them. Valentine and Proteus turn directly in the first scene from talk of travel to an exchange of puns; and the servants, Speed and Launce, are soon at it in their own different fashions. Wit belongs of course in such a world, but this early sample of it is dry and curiously spiritless. It is almost purely verbal. "Your old vice still," says Speed to Launce (III.i. 282); "mistake the word." Both masters and men, not to speak of Julia with her maid Lucetta, have caught it like the plague. It does not give them the gaiety which their successors in Shakespearean comedy will have, and which will never depend on puns for its expression, though puns will by no means disappear. There is in fact no gaiety in *The Two Gentlemen of Verona* outside of a few scenes dealing with the sensible Launce and his unwanted dog. Launce looks forward not merely to the Launcelot Gobbo whose name he suggests but to a whole line of clowns whose humor is in their hearts and stomachs rather than on their tongues. Speed looks backward to barrenness and will not thrive.

One of the interesting things about *The Two Gentlemen of Verona* is the studies it contains of things to come in Shakespeare. Julia is something like Portia when she discusses suitors with her maid (I.ii), and something like Viola when she discusses herself in disguise (IV.iv). Proteus tells almost as many lies as Bertram does in *All's Well That Ends Well*. The Friar Patrick at whose cell Silvia can arrange to meet Eglamour is soon, in *Romeo and Juliet,* to change his name to Laurence; and indeed there is already a Friar Laurence here (V.ii.37). And the forest near Mantua which Valentine finds so much more agreeable than "flourishing peopled towns" is a promise of Arden. But *The Two Gentlemen of Verona* is at best half-grown. Its seriousness is not mingled with its mirth. It has done a great deal in that it has set a scene and conceived an atmosphere. It has done no more.

Suggested References

The number of possible references is vast and grows alarmingly. (The *Shakespeare Quarterly* devotes a substantial part of one issue each year to a list of the previous year's work, and *Shakespeare Survey*—an annual publication—includes a substantial review of recent scholarship, as well as an occasional essay surveying a few decades of scholarship on a chosen topic.) Though no works are indispensable, those listed below have been found helpful.

1. Shakespeare's Times

Byrne, M. St. Clare. *Elizabethan Life in Town and Country*. Rev. ed. New York: Barnes & Noble, Inc., 1961. Chapters on manners, beliefs, education, etc., with illustrations.

Craig, Hardin. *The Enchanted Glass: the Elizabethan Mind in Literature*. New York and London: Oxford University Press, 1936. The Elizabethan intellectual climate.

Nicoll, Allardyce (ed.). *The Elizabethans*. London: Cambridge University Press, 1957. An anthology of Elizabethan writings, especially valuable for its illustrations from paintings, title pages, etc.

Shakespeare's England. 2 vols. Oxford: The Clarendon Press, 1916. A large collection of scholarly essays on a wide variety of topics (e.g., astrology, costume, gardening, horsemanship), with special attention to Shakespeare's references to these topics.

Tillyard, E. M. W. *The Elizabethan World Picture*. London: Chatto & Windus, 1943; New York: The Macmillan Company, 1944. A brief account of some Elizabethan ideas of the universe.

Wilson, John Dover (ed.). *Life in Shakespeare's England*. 2nd ed. New York: The Macmillan Company, 1913. An anthology of Elizabethan writings on the countryside, superstition, education, the court, etc.

2. Shakespeare

Bentley, Gerald E. *Shakespeare: A Biographical Handbook*. New Haven, Conn.: Yale University Press, 1961. The facts about Shakespeare, with virtually no conjecture intermingled.

Bradby, Anne (ed.). *Shakespeare Criticism, 1919–1935*. London: Oxford University Press, 1936. A small anthology of excellent essays on the plays.

Bush, Geoffrey Douglas. *Shakespeare and the Natural Condition*. Cambridge, Mass.: Harvard University Press; London: Oxford University Press, 1956. A short, sensitive account of Shakespeare's view of "Nature," touching most of the works.

Chambers, E. K. *William Shakespeare: A Study of Facts and Problems*. 2 vols. London: Oxford University Press, 1930. An invaluable, detailed reference work; not for the casual reader.

Chute, Marchette. *Shakespeare of London*. New York: E. P. Dutton & Co., Inc., 1949. A readable biography fused with portraits of Stratford and London life.

Clemen, Wolfgang H. *The Development of Shakespeare's Imagery*. Cambridge, Mass.: Harvard University Press, 1951. (Originally published in German, 1936.) A temperate account of a subject often abused.

Craig, Hardin. *An Interpretation of Shakespeare*. Columbia, Missouri: Lucas Brothers, 1948. A scholar's book designed for the layman. Comments on all the works.

Dean, Leonard F. (ed.). *Shakespeare: Modern Essays in Criticism*. New York: Oxford University Press, 1957. Mostly mid-twentieth-century critical studies, covering Shakespeare's artistry.

Granville-Barker, Harley. *Prefaces to Shakespeare.* 2 vols. Princeton, N.J.: Princeton University Press, 1946–47. Essays on ten plays by a scholarly man of the theater.

Harbage, Alfred. *As They Liked It.* New York: The Macmillan Company, 1947. A sensitive, long essay on Shakespeare, morality, and the audience's expectations.

Ridler, Anne Bradby (ed.). *Shakespeare Criticism, 1935–1960.* New York and London: Oxford University Press, 1963. An excellent continuation of the anthology edited earlier by Miss Bradby (see above).

Smith, D. Nichol (ed.). *Shakespeare Criticism.* New York: Oxford University Press, 1916. A selection of criticism from 1623 to 1840, ranging from Ben Jonson to Thomas Carlyle.

Spencer, Theodore. *Shakespeare and the Nature of Man.* New York: The Macmillan Company, 1942. Shakespeare's plays in relation to Elizabethan thought.

Stoll, Elmer Edgar. *Shakespeare and Other Masters.* Cambridge, Mass.: Harvard University Press; London: Oxford University Press, 1940. Essays on tragedy, comedy, and aspects of dramaturgy, with special reference to some of Shakespeare's plays.

Traversi, D. A. *An Approach to Shakespeare.* Rev. ed. New York: Doubleday & Co., Inc., 1956. An analysis of the plays, beginning with words, images, and themes, rather than with characters.

Van Doren, Mark. *Shakespeare.* New York: Henry Holt & Company, Inc., 1939. Brief, perceptive readings of all of the plays.

Whitaker, Virgil K. *Shakespeare's Use of Learning.* San Marino, Calif.: Huntington Library, 1953. A study of the relation of Shakespeare's reading to his development as a dramatist.

3. Shakespeare's Theater

Adams, John Cranford. *The Globe Playhouse*. Rev. ed. New York: Barnes & Noble, Inc., 1961. A detailed conjecture about the physical characteristics of the theater Shakespeare often wrote for.

Beckerman, Bernard. *Shakespeare at the Globe, 1599–1609*. New York: The Macmillan Company, 1962. On the playhouse and on Elizabethan dramaturgy, acting, and staging.

Chambers, E. K. *The Elizabethan Stage*. 4 vols. New York: Oxford University Press, 1923. Reprinted with corrections, 1945. An indispensable reference work on theaters, theatrical companies, and staging at court.

Harbage, Alfred. *Shakespeare's Audience*. New York: Columbia University Press; London: Oxford University Press, 1941. A study of the size and nature of the theatrical public.

Hodges, C. Walter. *The Globe Restored*. London: Ernest Benn, Ltd., 1953; New York: Coward-McCann, Inc., 1954. A well-illustrated and readable attempt to reconstruct the Globe Theatre.

Nagler, A. M. *Shakespeare's Stage*. Tr. by Ralph Manheim. New Haven, Conn.: Yale University Press, 1958. An excellent brief introduction to the physical aspect of the playhouse.

Smith, Irwin. *Shakespeare's Globe Playhouse*. New York: Charles Scribner's Sons, 1957. Chiefly indebted to J. C. Adams' controversial book, with additional material and scale drawings for model-builders.

Venezky, Alice S. *Pageantry on the Shakespearean Stage*. New York: Twayne Publishers, Inc., 1951. An examination of spectacle in Elizabethan drama.

4. Miscellaneous Reference Works

Abbott, E. A. *A Shakespearean Grammar*. New edition. New York: The Macmillan Company, 1877. An examination of differences between Elizabethan and modern grammar.

Bartlett, John. *A New and Complete Concordance . . . to . . . Shakespeare*. New York: The Macmillan Company, 1894. An index to most of Shakespeare's words.

Bullough, Geoffrey. *Narrative and Dramatic Sources of Shakespeare*. 4 vols. Vols. 5 and 6 in preparation. New York: Columbia University Press; London: Routledge & Kegan Paul, Ltd., 1957–. A collection of many of the books Shakespeare drew upon.

Greg, W. W. *The Shakespeare First Folio*. New York and London: Oxford University Press, 1955. A detailed yet readable history of the first collection (1623) of Shakespeare's plays.

Kökeritz, Helge. *Shakespeare's Names*. New Haven, Conn.: Yale University Press, 1959; London: Oxford University Press, 1960. A guide to the pronunciation of some 1,800 names appearing in Shakespeare.

————. *Shakespeare's Pronunciation*. New Haven, Conn.: Yale University Press; London: Oxford University Press, 1953. Contains much information about puns and rhymes.

Linthicum, Marie C. *Costume in the Drama of Shakespeare and His Contemporaries*. New York and London: Oxford University Press, 1936. On the fabrics and dress of the age, and references to them in the plays.

Muir, Kenneth. *Shakespeare's Sources*. London: Methuen & Co., Ltd., 1957. Vol. 2 in preparation. The first volume, on the comedies and tragedies, attempts to ascertain what books were Shakespeare's sources, and what use he made of them.

Onions, C. T. *A Shakespeare Glossary*. London: Oxford University Press, 1911; 2nd ed., rev., with enlarged addenda, 1953. Definitions of words (or senses of words) now obsolete.

Partridge, Eric. *Shakespeare's Bawdy*. Rev. ed. New York: E. P. Dutton & Co., Inc.; London: Routledge & Kegan Paul, Ltd., 1955. A glossary of bawdy words and phrases.

Shakespeare Quarterly. See headnote to Suggested References.

Shakespeare Survey. See headnote to Suggested References.

Smith, Gordon Ross. *A Classified Shakespeare Bibliography 1936–1958*. University Park, Pa.: Pennsylvania State University Press, 1963. A list of some 20,000 items on Shakespeare.

5. *The Two Gentlemen of Verona*

Brooks, Harold F. "Two Clowns in a Comedy (to Say Nothing of the Dog): Speed, Launce (and Crab) in *The Two Gentlemen of Verona*," *Essays and Studies 1963*, ed. S. Gorley Putt. London: John Murray, Ltd., 1963. Pp. 91–100.

Danby, John F. "Shakespeare Criticism and *Two Gentlemen of Verona*," *Critical Quarterly*, II (1960), 309–21.

Harrison, Thomas Perrin. "Concerning *The Two Gentlemen of Verona* and Montemayor's *Diana*," *Modern Language Notes*, XLI (1926), 251–52.

Latham, Grace. "On Julia, Silvia, Hero and Viola," *Transactions of the New Shakespeare Society*, Part IV (1887–1892), 319–50.

Nemerov, Howard. *Poetry and Fiction: Essays*. New Brunswick, New Jersey: Rutgers University Press, 1963.

Parks, George B. "The Development of *The Two Gentlemen of Verona*," *Huntington Library Bulletin*, No. 11 (1937), 1–11.

Parrott, Thomas Marc. *Shakespearean Comedy*. New York and London: Oxford University Press, 1949.

Pettet, E. C. *Shakespeare and the Romance Tradition*. London: Staples Press, Ltd., 1950.

Small, Samuel Asa. "The Ending of *The Two Gentlemen of Verona*," *Publications of the Modern Language Association*, XLVIII (1933), 767–76.